Tina Turner Bi

Extraordinary Journey and My Life

"*Sometimes you've got to let everything go – purge yourself. If you are unhappy with anything… Whatever is bringing you down, get rid of it. Because you'll find that when you're free, your true creativity, your true self comes out.*"

- Tina Turner -

By Shameka E Brown

TABLE OF CONTENTS

INTRODUCTION

How often do you get to paraphrase Voltaire, the French Enlightenment philosopher, in the context of rock and pop music? Here we go. It would have been necessary to create Tina Turner if she did not exist. And, surprisingly, that is exactly what happened in reality.

Anna Mae Bullock, the towering talent, was born on November 26, 1939, to a turbulent family in rural Nutbush, Tennessee, and grew up around the southeastern United States. She, like many other future soul music queens, learned to sing in the fervent respect of local Baptist church choirs. Also, like many other future funk divas, such as Aretha Franklin and Sharon Jones, Anna Mae didn't spend too much time in the prayer pews. She favored a new kind of soul-stirring beat, which she discovered in the secular swagger of rhythm and blues-infused soul and bluesy rock music.

Maps, however, are just pieces of paper, and it was quickly obvious to young Miss Bullock that dreams have no north or south, allowing her to gravitate, like so many others before her, into America's large northern urban centers, to places that seemed to be always waiting for a storm to happen. East St. Louis, Illinois, was just such a spot beyond any maps, and she was, indeed, a secret storm ready to be released, although still being in her early teen years. And it was there, sixteen years after her birth as Anna Mae, that she was recreated by an ambitious bandleader with a predilection for exploiting precious natural resources.

Tina Turner's most basic and obvious characteristic is that she is a master (or mistress) of sheer, unadulterated metamorphosis. What that something inside of her to which she alludes may be difficult to articulate in concrete words, but it can undoubtedly be detailed in detail. Yes, this core truth of her life, one of constant change, growth, and evolution, is simple, but it also helps to guide us through the twisting maze of a very complicated, at times contradictory, and multi-layered woman and artist.

She would eventually turn herself from a hot and heavy rhythm-and-blues-oriented soul singer into a rock star, a movie star, and a global feminine fame of goddess-like proportions by believing in that something inside her, even if she didn't know what to call it. Her mystique stems from her impoverished beginnings, her nightmare domestic relationship, and, most of all, her superhuman powers as an emotive singer, entertainer, and dancer.

But it was nearly as indefinable as her hoarse voice and as stunning as her unending legs that made her an icon of feminine survival and human victory. If I were to describe what she believed in, I'd have to go for the rhapsodic and maybe ambiguous: the idea of no constraints and the capacity to live one's fantasies on a daily basis. In that regard, she is also a radical dichotomy: a character that serves as an ambiguous symbol of suffering while simultaneously personifying success over physical and psychological adversity, as well as triumph over posttraumatic stress.

While she morphed herself several times over the course of her full-spectrum life, she also received some unexpected help from what we might call karma. But it came from an unexpected source, because she didn't transform from Anna Mae to Tina overnight or even entirely on her own. Certainly not.

Ike Turner's looming presence conferred both her name and the potential to make it as well-known as the weather, and heavy weather it was. That's why embodying a paradox is at the heart of her story, both her life story and her love story: her danger was also her mentor, a terrifying Svengali character of Phil Spector-scaled craziness. A chance meeting with Ike as a teenager impacted not just her life, but also the trajectory of musical history. Chance, it turns out, is a slang term for fate.

There are three things to know about the infamous name Ike Turner, and three reasons why he is still relevant even after a lengthy life of self-destructive infamy through drug abuse and domestic violence. One, in 1951, he recorded "Rocket 88," which is widely regarded as the first rock-and-roll song. Turner was the Kings of Rhythm's twenty-year-old leader at the time, and their rendition of a sped-up basic twelve-bar blues song, with Jackie Brenston on lead vocals, achieved number one in the charts while simultaneously igniting a complete musical revolution.

This, of course, before Elvis Presley, the white genius who stole Chuck Berry's raunchy black attitude, popularized it enormously, and drove us directly into the arms of the Beatles. Ike did indeed hear the future coming, loud and clear. Besides, Little Richard and Johnny Otis both claimed he did. And Ike signaled to get on board.

Two, he was a tormented talent himself: musician, bandleader, arranger, songwriter, talent scout, and record producer of considerable skill, particularly as the commanding leader of the Kings, until meeting a certain young tornado from Tennessee and forming his famed co-named Revue. You didn't have to like him — and few did — to admire his skills.

But we might assume that it is number three that keeps us saying his name today: he created Tina Turner. One night in 1957, while watching his band play at St. Louis' Club Manhattan, the diminutive teen Anna Mae Bullock approached the stage during an intermission and audaciously asked to sing with them, claiming that the bandleader's music "put her into a trance." Soon enough, she'd be putting all the rest of us in a trance, something we can only call that special jittery Tina Trance.

Ike and Tina Turner started their careers at the top of the pop game as a raucous but brilliant structural unit. This early praise was followed by a string of singles on several tiny labels, as well as one of the most demanding live performance touring schedules in music history.

Ike, ever the quick thinker, swiftly established a troupe of support vocalists for Tina nicknamed the Ikettes, while he remained as the puppet king mastermind playing balefully in the background.
With a production that matched the James Brown revue in terms of sheer sweaty spectacle, the group established a solid reputation that audience members quickly embraced as one of the hottest and potentially most explosive of all rock/pop ensembles. Between 1963

and 1966, with a bawdy female screamer filling the Brown hot star role, the band toured continually around the country despite the lack of a hit song, a tremendous accomplishment in and of itself, since they were powered by pure word of mouth and ear power.

Tina's fame quickly rose as a result of public appearances on American Bandstand and Shindig!, the era's equivalent of going viral.In 1965, the whole Revue spotlighted her on Hollywood a Go Go, the Andy Williams Show, and the Big TNT Show. This attracted not only a large white audience, but also a significant pop mainstream public awareness in general. She was prepared for the spotlight.

To ultimately solidify their international recognition, they appeared on the Ed Sullivan Show in 1970, which was perhaps the first major mass experience with Ike and Tina for music fans with light complexions like mine. They had reached a watershed moment in their careers not just by being commercially anointed by Sullivan, but also by transitioning from their previous rhythm-and-blues and soul music vibe to certified rock & roll, and then to rock music proper. They may have even contributed to the evolution of rock and roll into rock per se. At the very least, they established pop rock.

In a series of interviews with musicians, music critics, journalists, and broadcasters, I gleaned valuable insights into what makes Tina tick. My conversations with Aaron Cohen, the Chicago-based author of Move On Up: Soul Music and Black Cultural Power; James Porter, the broadcaster/author of Wild in the Streets, a history of the black origins of rock and roll and the evolution of black rock; and John Corcelli, a Toronto-based music journalist and author of Frank Zappa FAQ, who also kindly wrote the foreword to my book on Sharon Jones' soul music, have all been extremely fruitful in terms of exploring and unearthing the Their insights on what made Tina so remarkable proved invaluable in navigating the turbulent seas before, during, and after Hurricane Ike.

Ike Turner died in 2007 (he'd been dead inside for years), and at his funeral oration, the brilliant but completely insane master producer Phil Spector began his eulogy by proclaiming that Ike had made Tina into a gem. So far, so excellent, and entirely accurate. But then the psychopathic Phil (now an imprisoned murder felon) began to explain that any five other singers could have done what she did under his masterful tutelage, especially if they had been under his own Spectorized production sway, despite the fact that he had only produced a single song for her (albeit a very important song).

This could have been the first time the world realized the full extent of Spector's mental illness, because by then everyone on the planet knew not only what Tina was creatively capable of, but also what she had already accomplished on her own in the thirty years since escaping Ike's paranoid and coke-addled clutches. And here was Ike's third perplexing gift to musical history: the irony that his own compulsive possessiveness eventually drove née Bullock away from him and into the arms of a grateful global audience, into our arms.

But first, they shared and well-deserved stardom as a creative team, although a tortuous partnership on her part. They turned another professional corner with an up-tempo version of the Creedence Clearwater Revival song "Proud Mary," which forever altered the Turner landscape and made it clear who was truly leading the charge musically. It sold over a million copies and earned a Grammy nomination for best duo/group rhythm-and-blues performance. She was clearly spreading out both creatively and professionally, and she was certainly moving well beyond Ike.

Unsurprisingly, many younger listeners and readers who were enthralled by her spectacular solo career may be unfamiliar with their early collaborative work. By the mid-1970s, a confluence of factors was pushing the pair away from the duo format that had served them so well for more than a decade. Tina, of course, was developing her own confident image, while Ike had devolved into a terrible habit on Bolivian nasal cures, not to mention his spiraling anger against the budding Tina. Shows began to be canceled, and contracts were unsigned.

Tina filed for divorce and left his company, both emotionally and professionally, in 1976, claiming that her acceptance of Buddhist meditation and chanting techniques had helped her endure the horrors of their claustrophobic relationship at the time. She was dismayed to learn that by abandoning Ike in the middle of a concert tour, she was accountable to tour promoters for the canceled events. Their divorce was ultimately finalized in 1978, and she was finally free of the domineering impresario who had yet contributed to her becoming a household name, a name she paradoxically maintained as part of the court settlement.

Tina triumphantly returned to the stage in 1978, supported by United Artists management and supervised by a new manager, Roger Davies, who encouraged her to abandon the revue-format band and reinvent herself as a far grittier rock-and-roll performer. She went on a quick tour to establish her new persona, opening for the Rolling Stones and Rod Stewart (a guaranteed road to rock royalty), and then secured a new lucrative solo deal with Capitol Records. A globe tour in promotion of her new comeback album and image has begun.

Hollywood, predictably, beckoned once more. Tina Turner, the new and improved Tina Turner, had come. The rest is her story: a remarkable life and even more incredible music, both of which are hypnotic. The story of Tumult! is a lengthy examination of the fairly amazing transformation of meek Anna Mae Bullock into the force of nature we know today as Tina Turner. Turner is, of course, the story of someone who was already waiting to emerge, not a Svengali-guided Pygmalion creature at all, but a fully formed if vulnerable young lady who was bound to burst out of the claustrophobic shell imposed on her one way or another. And, Lordy, did she burst out.

Turner is currently simmering on the back burner of mortality's stove, having battled intestinal cancer (the same disease that claimed the lives of two other soul goddesses, Sharon Jones in 2016 and Aretha Franklin in 2018) and having undergone a kidney transplant that was rejected and was followed by numerous seizures and strokes. Her powerful voice and brilliantly athletic figure may have been silenced by this ailment, but her genuine legacy is only now coming into focus: that deep belief in her interior talent that could never be destroyed.

Even if mortality takes her away, as it looks it must, her spirit has just been muffled, not completely muted. And the audio artifacts, recordings, concerts, movies, and films she left behind continue to amplify that energy. Tumult! follows in the footsteps of my previous books on two remarkable female musicians (Back to Black: Amy Winehouse's Only Masterpiece and Long Slow Train: The Soul Music of Sharon Jones and the Dap-Kings, both published by Backbeat Books in 2016 and 2018, respectively). I aim to avoid the soap opera struggles as much as possible, save where necessary for the plot, in favor of a deep dive into her creative wellspring and lofty achievements in musical creativity.

Even the intricacies of her horrific early pre-solo years influenced the idea and production of her subsequent work. Exult!—which could also be a fitting subtitle for her story. Tumult! But, considering her early and middle beginnings, it just feels natural. In general, it conjures up images of adoring rock stadiums, as well as change, turmoil, upheaval, ferment, uproar, commotion, ruckus, frenzy, and turbulence, which are frequently connected with convulsions, tempests, storms, and maelstroms. All of these adjectives are easily associated with what happens when Tina Turner begins to work her magic on a crowd.

However, exult may be as suitable to her, particularly in the long post-Ike upheaval era we now associate with her name: to feel or express triumphant exhilaration or gladness, to rejoice, to be joyful, to be ecstatic, to revel in, to be entranced, and, probably most importantly, to be proud. And, like one of the songs most frequently associated with her career, Proud Tina keeps rolling.

In the instance of this one-of-a-kind global superstar, we have a case study in sheer creative willpower, and her achievements were lofty by any and all artistic and commercial criteria. Singer, composer, dancer, actor, icon: she rose to international notoriety as the featured singer in the Ike and Tina Turner Revue, but she then far surpassed that recognition with a new astronomically apparent solo career wholly of her own creation. Fate would even later apologize to her for the error it made with her the first time, bringing in a new and considerably improved love interest, Erwin Bach, almost as if to make up.

She has sold more than 200 million records and is often referred to as the Queen of Rock and Roll. She has received eight Grammy Awards from twenty-five nominations, three Hall of Fame Awards, and a Grammy Lifetime Achievement Award; she was inducted into the Rock and Roll Hall of Fame in 1991; and she also received Kennedy Center Honors in 2005.

My book begins its understanding of her truly transcending popular appeal as a rock star and pop music goddess, rather than just as a soul, funk, or rhythm-and-blues musician. I believe — and have always believed — that pop music is a major creative and cultural artifact, reflecting our planetary cultures in a way that is often underestimated simply because of the massive monetary success levels at stake among the higher tiers of pop musicians.

Tina is often regarded less seriously as an artist simply because she has sold more live concert tickets than any other solo singer in music history, according to Guinness World Records. But, more importantly for me, how her songs were recorded so efficiently is what caused them to be presented so passionately. Her albums' studio, band, and production standards are all supernaturally fine in their support of her craft.

In many ways, she was "a spy in the house of love," as early feminist novelist Anais Nin put it, sending back dispatches from the front lines of the heart showing the dynamics of human relationships, usually the kind involving abundant pain blended with inevitable success. It was a signature look she had developed as a survivor.

Being Tina Turner needed a lot of stamina, and as the consummate love spy, she shared a particularly obscure skill with other professionals in emotional espionage. Hers is an extraordinary ability for survival, which I can best describe using a term from Ben Macintyre's book A Spy Among Friends. She was frail in form, but her soul was built of a tensile, almost impossible-to-break material that never shattered or even bent in its confidence.

So much for Tumult!We attempt to take her seriously as an artist and figure out what extraordinary abilities she possessed that allowed her to connect with so many of her fellow mortals on such a profound heart-to-heart level. She is, in reality, a human heart pumping in high heels.

CHAPTER 1:
The Myth of Origin

Tina Turner's lesser-known album is also one of her most significant and revealing. "Nutbush City Limits" is a song by Ike Turner that was published in 1973 as a single and on an album of the same name while she was still working with him as her partner and producer. It isn't her most adored album, nor is it her most popular song. It was, however, a watershed moment, even a Turner Point, because it was the first song she composed by herself, for herself, and for herself. It was a tremendous hit for the prolific couple, who had been successful and adored for more than a decade yet were still only three years away from her divorce and hard-won independence.

It was also a song of deep intimacy, sentiment, and personal nostalgia in which she celebrated her rural roots in a frank and honest manner. It was so meaningful to her that she would release various updated versions of it over the years, most notably a live recording in 1988, several dance remixes in 1991, and yet another rerecording in 1993, long after she had become a stellar solo performer and a megastar in her own right. This raucously danceable ballad evidently meant a lot to her. The underlying reality behind the song was, of course, that it was always her who made the couple's music special from the start, which must have irritated her insecure and temperamental husband.

This simple little tune was practically a special type of national anthem for the rural village of Nutbush, Tennessee, a place barely anybody knew existed other than Anna Mae Bullock, the future Tina, who resided there. But the song is also essential in the way it situates and embeds her origins in a way that would never leave her, no matter how much fame or fortune came her way. It was far from Interstate 40, dropped by an obviously sardonic inventor in the middle of nowhere between Jackson and Memphis, but close enough to Highway 19 to make it the escape route for any bored person looking for bigger and freer horizons.

This simple song extols and elevates, even mythologizes, a place and period that will remain in the heart of a southern girl like Miss

Bullock for the rest of her life. And, despite its simple message of home and hearth, "Go to the store on Fridays, go to church on Sundays," .."It is nonetheless propelled along in a full-charging manner, fueled by Ike's admittedly quick arrangements and his own powerful throbbing electric organ and twanging guitar playing, both paired with their Kings of Rhythm's customary swaying swagger."

The 1973 song was clearly ironic, perhaps even schizoid, considering the lifestyle she was trapped in at the time of writing it: being forced onstage each night despite health issues such as bronchitis leading to tuberculosis, a collapsed right lung and infected legs, and a permanently bruised jaw from Ike's abuse, as Nick Hasted effectively described it in Classic Rock. She described it as "living in hell's domain," and Hasted lamented her allegation that she was "brainwashed" during that time.

It must have felt like she was trapped in a cult: "Her nightmare parody of suburban domestic bliss required her to treat Ike like a king while caring for their four children, and the musical life that once inspired her wasn't much better." On stage, the once blisteringly inspiring Ike and Tina Turner Revue could now be a sad, exhausted spectacle." So, perhaps it was natural for her lonely imagination to return to her idealized country memories of the quiet hamlet where she first saw the light of day in the midst of the Ike cult.

Of fact, while she was clearly using her hometown motif as a survival mechanism until the ramifications of her own personal Stockholm syndrome could be avoided, neither Nutbush nor her upbringing in general were ideal. It most likely appeared that way to Ike. Nutbush is an unincorporated rural settlement in Haywood County, Tennessee's westernmost county. It was founded in the early nineteenth century by European American settlers who brought with them enslaved African Americans to labor on the region's plantations. Those forced African American migrants erected houses and churches that still survive today.

Historically, the town had been dedicated to the production and harvesting of cotton, a commodity crop since the antebellum period, when its processing and transportation relied on institutionalized enslavement. Other renowned musicians arose from this odd locale, including some well-known blues recording artists such as Hambone Willie Newbern, Noah Lewis, and the legendary Sleepy John Estes. There's also a famous line dance called the Nutbush that still exists and was even featured in an episode of the television show Glee. Nutbush was the blues personified.

Her immediate family included her mother, Zelma Priscilla, and father, Floyd Richard Bullock, two mismatched souls who happened to be married to each other, as well as two older sisters, Evelyn Juanita and Ruby Alline. Anna Mae's extended family of maternal and paternal grandparents raised her in Nutbush and neighboring Ripley after her birth in nearby Brownsville (where her actual delivery took place, at the Haywood Memorial Hospital, a tiny municipal building whose basement was set aside for the care of black patients).

That bigger clan also includes a significant and separate maternal lineage from Anna Mae. Joseph, a sharecropper, and Georgiana Currie, her mother Zelma's parents, were from separate dispossessed cultures that both formed a tragic but vital part of American history. He was three-quarters Navajo, and his wife, Anna Mae's grandmother, was three-quarters Cherokee, the first people whose ancestral lands had been confiscated during Tennessee's formation. They were both one-quarter black.

This could explain some of the exotically alluring qualities that I've always found most fascinating about Tina's future: a sharply marked Native heritage as strong as her own stunning cheekbones. Kurt Loder's portrayal of her when he helped her write the first of her two memoirs has always stuck with me. Her sisters and cousin wore their hair in tight plaits, as is customary for young black daughters, whereas Anna Mae has "undone her mother's patient braidwork and gathered her full reddish hair into a rough ponytail at the back, revealing an exotic facial geography of elegant broad bones, richly sculpted lips, honey-toned skin, smooth as a breezeless sea, and eyes like tiny brown beacons."

Anna Mae would be integrated into this mix of transported African migrants pushed into slavery and the ruins of a once great nation of

Native inhabitants. She would be born into a world of conflict and trauma, both in her immediate domestic family life of continually fighting parents at war with each other for unclear reasons, and on a larger scale in the globe at large, a world at war for equally dubious causes.

On November 26, 1939, two months before her birth, England and France declared war on Nazi Germany, which had invaded Poland with Soviet acquiescence if not explicit support. Tumult was already active in the world around her, waiting to fully erupt within. Hello and welcome to your childhood.

Unfortunately for Anna Mae, while she felt some warmth at her grandparents' home, she felt none on her own because her parents, Richard and Zelma, seemed to have no time or energy to care for their youngest daughter following their regular battles. She definitely felt like an unwanted kid, which she was, for her sister Alline had been born into a marriage that had yet to devolve into open domestic violence.

This left Anna Mae with plenty of alone time, which she spent traveling around the natural backcountry realm beyond the home, if only to escape the fierce storms that raged within its gloomy walls. Along with her broad psychic survival of potential parental injury at any time, whether from violence or neglect, her own claim on that enigmatic energy within her that permitted an outsized optimism and hopefulness was equally astonishing.

Her father's position on Poindexter farm as the leader or manager (legally labeled as overseer) of the other sharecroppers meant she didn't remember being poor (maybe a basic and simple life would be more true). Of course, the rigorous southern social strata had an impact on her in terms of segregation, but it was seemingly just the way of the world to a young girl, incapable of comprehending why her kind of people were accepted as long as they knew and kept their place.

Apart from walking the meadows and streams, her only joy was attending enormous BBQ picnics with live music on occasion. It wasn't really blues, more like country music at the time, but it thrilled her to see a live band of revelers shouting it up and making a joyful noise, at least until the picnic was finished. The music's end was unfortunate since it meant she had to return indoors to a mother who didn't speak with her and a father who she was certain didn't want her around at all. Her only companion was music.

She used to think the difficulty was because she heard her mother had snatched her father from another girl, not because she loved him but out of spite. So it was plain, even to a young girl, that the reason they didn't get along was simply that they didn't like, let alone love, each other. Even at this early point of life, it's difficult not to hear the faint echo of a future long-distant song, "what's love but a second hand emotion, who needs a heart when a heart can be broken?"'"

She also had to deal with allegations that she was not only unwanted because her parents were unhappy, but that she was actually not her father's child at all and that, before her birth, her father's sister Martha Mae and her husband had been living with her parents. Martha was rumored to be having an affair with another man, and Anna Mae was that man's child, not Richard's. Then, when she came, looking nothing like her dark-skinned sister Alline (her self-description in memory was of a "red kid," fair-skinned and fair-haired), the local community, who were "church people," didn't like much for her either.

Growing up, the only thing she could rely on was her elder sister's love, despite the fact that they were temperamentally unlike Alline being more quiet and deliberate, while Anna Mae was wild to the core from the start. In the end, she was always left to her own solitary devices, constantly busy, running, moving, and doing things: turbulent from the start, feeling somewhat like a complete outsider (which she undoubtedly was spiritually), and simply wandering out on her own, almost joyfully sequestered. Is it any surprise, then, that given the nasty energy environment she grew up in, she may be vulnerable enough to be compromised later in her own poisonous domestic tangle?

And this catastrophic forthcoming turn of events would come when she was still a teenager, meeting a man eight years her older, a man with a band playing live music, but also one with a dark side. Of course, the difference between her parents' tangle and her own is that she had a rare opportunity to use her inherent skills in a liberating way: to sing, sing, sing. When it came to her difficult background, though, she maintained her generally upbeat demeanor.

"I didn't dwell on it," she told Loder of Rolling Stone in 1986. "I had my own world, my own thing going on." I had to forge my own path. I had to go out into the world and become strong in order to realize my life's destiny." destiny completed, I believe.

"My struggle began at birth, when I entered the world as Anna Mae Bullock," Turner said to Deborah Davis and Dominik Wichmann, the authors who helped her compile her adult memories in "My Love Story, thirty-two years later. I've spent my entire life fighting my way through an environment of negative karma. "There was a shadow hanging over my earliest years, cast by someone more absent than present, my mother." The question of how it felt to be an unwanted child, and, more remarkably, how that child prevailed in spite of the many strikes against her, forms the foundation of her character, her later persona, and her life's convoluted narrative in general.

Indeed, this woman's first childhood memory was of her parents fighting, an interpersonal dynamic that had to have stubbornly lodged itself in her consciousness. The ultimate irony is that she later found herself in the same type of loveless and threatening relationship. And yet, this strange combination of her private power and personal weakness was eventually portrayed publicly in her frequently revealing lyrics of love and sorrow, allowing the entire world to feel her pain.

Even if youngsters discover a way to escape adversity by living in their own world—especially the preternaturally brilliant ones before sharing their talents with the rest of us—the larger world outside continues to spin unabated. Because Anna Mae was born into conflict and trauma, the greater world continued to mirror her troubled home life, with entire countries standing in for parental clashes. Just as Europe was slipping into armed conflict two months before she was born, the entire globe was immersed in a war more dreadful than any before it two years later.

Japan's sudden attack on Hawaii in December 1941 sparked a rapid and decisive response, driving the entire world into a devastating frenzy of nationalist fervor that strangely also affected the Bullock family directly. When a new army site emerged in Oak Ridge, Tennessee, near Knoxville, a sudden wartime employment boom related to the military economy and defense plants arose, one that was especially beneficial for formerly struggling black inhabitants eager for work.

Richard and Zelma Bullock were enticed by the potential of new jobs as well as a long-awaited opportunity to leave Nutbush, but they decided to depart together rather than individually, leaving their already neglected family behind. Government positions evidently appealed to them more than farmwork ever did, and even though they disliked each other, both seemed to resent, if not actually loathe, their children, none of whom were ever truly loved or cared for.

Alline was assigned to the Native side of the family, while Anna Mae was assigned to "Mama" Roxanna and Alex Bullock, her father's austere religious parents, the four deacons and deacons of the Woodlawn Missionary Baptist Church, much to her chagrin. It would put her off to traditional deity worship for the rest of her life, possibly leading her to seek her own spiritual alternatives. But the gospel music she heard in the sacred church environment was a different story: the furious music inspired by faith was something she could completely relate to.

I like to refer to certain performers by the seemingly contradictory moniker gospel funk. Aaron Cohen, music historian and author of Move On Up, a history of soul music, agrees with me that this certainly mysterious category in music is real and tangible: the notion that sacred music underwent significant stylistic innovations but remained at its core a boisterous expression of fervor merely shifted from faith into funk.

"There is definitely gospel funk—check out the two Numero Group compilations under the Good God! label!" title (despite the fact that these collated records are from after Tina Turner's ascension). At this point, I'm not sure Tina Turner veered too much from her contemporaries or influences in terms of converting the beat and repertoire of gospel into R&B, just by changing the lyrics."

True, he's referring to the transformation of "Lord" into "Lover," a recursive change from gospel to soul that also requires a shift in attention, sometimes even transposing Lord into Ike. But it was always and significantly the religious vibe that moved her during her formative years. Aside from hearing popular music on her mother's radio and attending communal picnics, her first live musical influences were sacred, as she stated in her Woman in Rock Rolling Stone entry identifying her influences: "Well, it was a church person in the early days, Mahalia Jackson, and Rosetta Tharpe." These spiritual and extremely loud voices I knew were known and respected figures in the black race. But I must admit that I've always covered male singers' songs. I haven't listened to a lot of women's music."

In Joe Smith's book Off the Record, she mentions singing some of the McGuire Sisters songs she listened to as a little girl when she was frequently broken-hearted, implying she was already singing the blues. It was as easy to her as speaking: "It makes me remember just how long I have really been singing."

Wild in the Streets: Tales from Rock and Roll's Negro Leagues, a forthcoming book on black rock music from Northwestern University Press, spoke eloquently to me about Tina Turner's place in the pantheon of both great black rockers in general and exemplary black female pop artists in particular. He agreed with me that she carried a significant degree of gospel anger into her propulsive funk sound, but he also highlighted that she was always essentially a practitioner of soul music, no matter how widely her musical interests diverged.

"Yes, Tina is still classified as a soul singer." I certainly believe so. Despite all of her stylistic shifts, she never lost her churchy R&B

vibe. Depending on the circumstances, she may have accentuated it with more rawness or sophistication, but the soul sense was always at the heart of it all with her."

Once her community learned how easily she vocalized, the young Anna Mae was requested to join the local church choir, and at the age of nine or ten, she was especially fond of doing the cheerful fast-tempo hymns, quite ready, it seemed, to be a tiny star and shout about paradise even then. Her sister noticed her dancing so fast to gospel music that her underwear would slip to her feet without her noticing. She was always ready to offer drama, and she used to return home from the movies and act out scenes for her family, stretching out on the floor to show how starlets died on film. Melodrama appeared to appeal to her personality.

By the age of thirteen, she had become an unintentional orphan due to her parents' disdain for each other as well as their lack of emotional capacity to care for their children. She supplemented her income by working as a maid for Guy and Connie Henderson, a friendly neighborhood family (i.e., people who truly liked each other), once jokingly telling McCall's magazine, "I went to work for a nice white family as a maid." I was similar to their younger daughter. Besides cooking, the Hendersons taught me a lot about being a woman. I learnt how to care for their baby, so when I had mine, I was already prepared."

The parental divorce lasted through Anna Mae's formative school years at Flagg Grove Elementary School until the ninth grade, when she began singing in the church chorus at Nutbush's Spring Hill Baptist Church. Family trauma accelerated when her mother abruptly departed for a period, finally seeking freedom from her abusive father. The future echoes are hard to miss here, with Anna Mae herself eventually having to flee precisely the same kind of emotionally terrifying dynamic that had spawned her.

Even as good as the Hendersons were to her, they couldn't teach her everything, such as how to avoid being with the wrong man. It occurs to me that her future husband, like most cunning abusers, would rapidly learn how to exploit and capitalize on her clear childhood abandonment issues and use her severe isolated vulnerability to his fullest advantage.

Remember, this was just three years after she mistakenly ventured into East St. Louis's "The Hole" district with her older sister as an ignorant guide to the nightlife. Thus, when Anna Mae was sixteen, her grandmother died, and she was transported to the city to reportedly warmly reconcile with her sister and wayward mother, the next seismic shift occurred for the self-professed tomboy country girl.

And there was another surprise waiting for her in St. Louis, a massive city with equally large music and entertainment districts that must have appeared like another planet compared to Nutbush: the young girl's fateful encounter with Ike Turner. This was the obnoxious man who would loom so large in her life tale, creating both a nightmare of domestic déjà vu while also strangely offering an enlivening entry into her genuine calling in that life.

And now for one of the most bizarre twists in the Tina tragedy. While Ike was most likely a psychopath—or, at the absolute least, a sexist sociopath—it's also true that Tina would not exist without him, his music, and their original sixteen-year working relationship. Nobody knows what would have happened to Anna Mae Bullock if Turner hadn't stepped into her karma field at just the perfect moment to move it a few degrees more to the direction of her dreams.

My theory is that Anna Mae not only exists, but has always been right in front of our eyes and ears, mimicking Tina Turner. And what a magnificent impression she's left us with of an ultimately soaring creative creature, a sheer wild pagan goddess unleashed on all of our senses at once. And if Tina can be legitimately defined as the hardest-working lady in show industry (to use a phrase from James Brown), which I believe we can all agree she is, then Ike was the meanest man in show business.

Nonetheless, Ike's obviously strange legacy includes the odd fact that he gave us Tina, for which we should all be eternally grateful. Hell, I'm sure she's grateful in some manner, since she knows what it's like to be given a once-in-a-lifetime opportunity to shine in the spotlight. Once again, chance is a slang term for fate.

Apart from his evident musical, arranging, and band-leading abilities, which were great, I will argue that he was brought to Earth for his exceptional aptitude as a talent scout, for which he should be justly remembered. Izear Luster "Ike" Turner Jr. lived from November 5, 1931, to December 12, 2007, and he had one of the oddest lives imaginable—almost as strange as Tina's, if not quite as inspiring. He started playing guitar and keyboard when he was eight years old and would have been called a creative prodigy if he hadn't been insane. Even though he was insane, his talents of creation were immense, just like his subsequent terrible appetites.

Turner, properly defined by Mojo magazine's editor Phil Alexander as "the cornerstone of modern-day rock and roll," was born in Clarksdale, Mississippi, to seamstress Beatrice Cushenbury and Baptist minister Isaiah (or Izear) Luster Turner. Turner frequently told the story of his father being set on and beaten by a white crowd (which he claimed to have observed), leaving him an invalid for three years before succumbing to his injuries, yet, like with other Ike legends, it should be regarded with a grain of salt.

According to blues historian Ted Drozdowski, Isaiah perished in an industrial accident. In any case, it resulted in his mother remarrying a man called Philip Reeves, a violent alcoholic with whom Ike frequently argued and fought physically, once knocking his stepfather out with a piece of wood and escaping to Memphis. They reunited later in life, presumably after each had expended all of their mutual fury. The scenario does, however, allow us to speculate on the psychological impact of such a domestic environment on young Ike Jr., and we don't have to be Freud to wonder about his personal history when it comes to sexual experiences and the often contradictory impulses: to love and to destroy.

He has described how a middle-aged lady named Miss Boozie "introduced" him to sex when he was six years old. When he walked past her house on his way to school, she would welcome him in to feed her chickens and then take him to bed, a routine that lasted for years. He stated that these meetings had not scarred him, remarking wryly to Celebrity Café that "today they would call it child molesting, to me I was just having fun," as told to Dominick Miserandino for a Hall of Famer biographical piece. He appears to have been raped twice by different women before the age of twelve, and was apparently a favorite of questionably adjusted ladies.

He began hanging out at the local Clarksdale radio station, WROX, at the age of eight, one of the few stations known to employ a black DJ, a unique figure known as Early Wright. Another deejay, John Frisella, decided to put the rambunctious boy to work spinning platters, which Ike described as "the beginning of his thing with music." Before long, he was left alone to play records while the adult deejay went across the street for a coffee and a cigarette. Freedom of expression and poor impulse control loomed prominently in his story from the start.

After this strange initiation, he was offered the formal job of deejay for the late afternoon shift by the station manager a few years later, while still a young teen, a role that meant he had quick and personal access to all new record releases before anyone else saw or heard them. Even at this early stage, he was noted for his devotion to a wide range of musical styles, frequently juxtaposing unexpected combinations of songs (such as boogie combined with rockabilly) in a form that is now known as mashups. Of course, there was no word for it back then.

During a disastrous visit to his buddy Ernest Lane's house, he happened to hear the famed Pinetop Perkins playing piano on his friend's father's instrument, which seemed to have ignited an already blossoming love of and intense curiosity about music. Even as a child, he seemed to be good at deception, convincing his mother to pay for piano lessons, but instead of taking them, he squandered the money at pool halls and went to his friend Ernest's house to watch and listen to Pinetop play alone in an audience of two. There are, of course, worse ways to study music than at the feet of a boogie-woogie icon.

He subsequently learned himself to play the guitar by listening to old blues albums, and in the 1940s, he moved into the Clarksdale Riverside Hotel, which was operated by an amicable lady who didn't rape him but did expose him to a slew of visiting musicians who stayed there. Giants like blues monarch Sonny Boy Williamson II and jazz titan Duke Ellington, with whom he would play music while they were traveling through town, were among the luminaries that passed through the hotel he shared with them on the road. Again, there are worse ways to learn about the power of rhythm than by hanging out with Duke and drinking.

Demonstrating the same kind of supernatural maturity (musically, not emotionally) as other young, gifted history makers, such as Lennon and McCartney, Jagger and Richards, and others, all of whom began playing together while still in high school (something he never paid much attention to), he joined a local rhythm ensemble, as they were then known, called the Tophatters, which included a few of his youthful friends: Raymond Hill, Eugene Fox, and others. Turner, who could not read music, studied his parts by listening to records at home and then performing them live on stage. The daring youngster was full of guts.

The Tophatters were a large band, and half of them wanted to play jazz while the other half wanted to play blues and boogie music, so they split up: one group called themselves the Dukes of Swing, and the other, Turner's portion, called themselves the Kings of Rhythm, a band name Turner kept for the rest of his long career. At one point in their early career, blues icon BB King heard them play and recommended them to the legendary Sam Phillips at Sun Studio (recording home of Elvis Presley and Jerry Lee Lewis, among others).

At this point, he was also honing his craft by accompanying Sonny Boy Williamson II, Howlin' Wolf, Elmore James, Muddy Waters, and Little Walter on stage for up to twelve hours. They played without intermission or breaks, so whenever one of the guys needed to take a rest, another band member had to step in and take his instrument. According to the Austin Chronicle, "that's how I learned to play drums and guitar as well as piano; if someone needed to go to the restroom, someone else had to take his place so the music could continue."

It hurts me to say this about a young man who subsequently developed into such a terrible monster, yet the young man was also a confirmed genius! At this period, the twenty-year-old artist recorded the groundbreaking song "Rocket 88" (called after a new model of Oldsmobile), an act that was the equivalent of Edison's invention of the lightbulb in rock music circles (which didn't really exist yet). It featured vocals by his band's saxophonist Jackie Brenston, as well as Turner on a lively boogie piano and giving an introduction that was eventually lifted note for note by none other than the great Little Richard for his future "Good Golly Miss Molly" success. They claim that geniuses usually borrow from the best.

While Ike and his Kings of Rhythm have been credibly identified as a watermark in the creative invention and popular distribution of the musical style known as rock and roll during their brief recording and performing period with Brenston, that uniquely hybrid mutation of several genres bent together in a raunchy romp had actually been slowly gestating for many, many years. Although it happened to appear at the same time in the late 1940s in America, it was already an old and nearly ancient term and style by pop music standards.

From the start, it was widely understood, at least among music fans, that the word "rock and roll" was a euphemism for the sex act, which had long been active in both jazz and blues folklore traditions. Several musical motifs, including vocal jazz (also a slang term for sex), blues (a secular brand of gospel shouting with a lover replacing the deity), swing, jitterbug, boogie-woogie, and rhythm and blues, were already old when they still felt new.

There was also a significant influx of country music in the early days of rock, including Ike's rockabilly, and later, when the Beatles fused the black music of artists they admired, such as Chuck Berry and Little Richard, with the seminal influence of Elvis Presley, then sprinkled in a dash of their own British skiffle origins, they propelled the style all the way into the rock age. However, its origins were more innocently mocking, with seamen singing sea chanteys, such as

Johnny Bowker's bawdy nineteenth-century ballad about his sweetheart requesting that he rock and roll her over.

1951 was a fantastic year for us for a variety of reasons. After a few decades of this fusion music known as rhythm and blues, mostly made for black audiences, Alan Freed, a corrupt radio deejay based in Cleveland, Ohio, began to play this music for mixed audiences in that year, while also coining the term "rock and roll" for the style. However, this mystery pattern was already in the popular media and popular among people of all nationalities, albeit without an official label or title. But, just as multiple people invented the lamp (both Tesla and Edison) and multiple people invented the radio (both Tesla and Marconi), multiple people invented rock and roll.

The Columbia Quartette used the phrase in a recording of "The Camp Meeting Jubilee" around 1900, with the expressed desire to "keep on rockin' and rollin' in your arms," denoting spiritual rapture; in 1922, blues singer Trixie Smith recorded "My Man Rocks Me (with One Steady Roll)," the first time the terms were used in a secular context; in 1932, the phrase "rock and roll" was heard in a Hal Roach film;

In 1938, Sister Rosetta Tharpe, a visionary gospel screamer who influenced both Chuck Berry and Tina Turner's subsequent styles, recorded "Rock Me," originally a gospel song by Thomas Dorsey called "Hide Me in Thy Bosom," in a secular "city" electric guitar blues manner. These songs and many others, including the boogie styles of Pete Johnson and Pinetop Perkins, Ike Turner's early mentor, were usually considered "race music" at the time; however, when Freed began broadcasting highly experimental tunes over his WJW AM station in Cleveland in 1951, he mixed and matched a slew of styles into his musical blender. Both he and the station's owner, Leo Mintz (who also happened to run a record store, in true Freed flair), referred to the music they promoted with the now-famous phrase "rock and roll."

"Rock and roll was an inevitable outgrowth of the social and musical interactions between black and whites in the South and Southwest," writes rock music historian Robert Palmer, whose books Rock Begins and Church of the Sonic Guitar are considered bibles on the subject. Its roots are a tangled mess. Bedrock black church music influenced blues, rural blues influenced white folk song and Northern ghetto black popular music, blues and back pop influenced jazz, and so on. The influence of black music on white music, however, was the single most crucial process."

Thus, a straight (if jittery) line can be made from a historic artist and performer like Ike Turner to the Beatles and the Rolling Stones and beyond, just as an equally straight but curvy one can be drawn from Tina Turner to Beyoncé and Nicki Minaj. When Ike Turner launched "Rocket 88" on March 5, 1951, he set off a secret storm that would last for years. Bill Haley would re-record the song a year later, in one of the first white covers of a black rhythm-and-blues song and possibly the first recording to feature Ike's guitarist, Willie Kizart, on distorted fuzzy feedback guitar.

Ike used to have a young Jimi Hendrix playing very fuzzy guitar with him at one point, but he let him go because Jimi's blazing solos were "aimless and went on way too long." He had an uncanny knack for identifying and utilizing the raw skills of those around him, even if he was a little too conservative to fully allow his players to rock on out of limits. But, for me, Ike's tonal force and powerful energy were the first truly rocking rock-and-roll numbers, unleashing a primal force that would only be amplified by his later discovery of the perfect lead singer, Anna Mae Bullock.

KING OF RHYTHM, IKE TURNER. "ROCKET 88" AMERICAN LEGION HALL, CHATTANOOGA, TENNESSEE, JULY 4, 1951

This iconic song's first known performance occurred only four months after its initial publication. I recently came upon a vintage poster for this show, which was displayed like an exhibit in a dream museum and described in reverent tones. It gave an authentic relic, almost as if it were the Holy Grail for some collectors of musical historical relics. As printed in the Hake's Auction House pamphlet, this unique item for sale also included a $4,000 price tag and a description that could almost be at home in a ritzy archaeology catalog: a "22x28.25" cardboard poster advertising a "Big 4th of July

Dance" at the American Legion Hall in Chattanooga Wed. July 4, 1951.

"Jackie Brenston" photo on the left with added text, "Singing 'Rocket 88' Featuring Ike Turner, King of the Ivories." "This show was less than four months after 'Rocket 88' was released by Chess Records in 1951," the auction listing said. The song is widely regarded as the first rock 'n' roll hit, reaching No. 1 on the Billboard R&B chart." The fact that "Rocket 88" was recorded in Memphis by Sam Phillips, who placed it with Chess Records for release, and Phillips used the money to launch his famed Memphis company Sun Records adds another "layer" to the tremendous history this piece represents. As a result, it is a significant artifact from the early days of rock 'n' roll.

For many of us, the really important historical "layer" here is that Phillips went on to found Sun with the profits from this song, allowing us to eventually hear Carl Perkins, Elvis Presley, Johnny Cash, Jerry Lee Lewis, Roy Orbison, Charlie Rich, and Conway Twitty (aka Harold Jenkins), among many others. According to legend, Turner was only paid $20 for the first recording, which he would never forget. His band at the time, officially known as Jackie Brenston and His Delta Cats, included Ike Turner on piano, Brenston on vocals and saxophone, Willie Bad Boy Sims on drums, Willie Kizart on fuzz guitar, and a young Raymond Hill, who would soon become Tina Turner's father.

James Porter, a professional listener and black rock historian, shares my strong admiration for the humanity-challenged Ike Turner despite his apparent personal problems. Some of us compared his musical discoveries to Picasso's (another misogynist monster) graphical breakthroughs in painting. "The evolution of Ike and/or Tina into a rock act is an interesting one," Porter argues. Ike, for his part, contributed to the creation of rock and roll as we know it with his involvement with Jackie Brenston's 1951 smash 'Rocket 88.' Willie Kizart's distorted guitar on this jump-blues classic was kept to rhythm, never taking a solo, yet his riffage propelled the tune like the V-8 engine cranked up the Oldsmobile that Brenston sang about. Even if Ike Turner had stopped making music after 'Rocket 88,' his rock and roll credentials would have been confirmed right then and there."

The Kings of Rhythm must be one of the longest-running acts in the music industry, much like rock, having performed in various forms for almost 65 years. Turner would bring Kizart, Sims, O'Neal, Jessie Knight, and one of Ike's first wives, Anne Mae Wilson, with him to East St. Louis, where his story as we know it today begins. Ike found the severe small weather phenomenon known as a Bullock storm there, and they began to enchant the Missouri clubgoers at the hot little Club Manhattan.

As is customary, chance reigns supreme. Turner's first single sold over 500,000 copies, causing ego clashes within the band and resulting in Brenston's departure and a brief hiatus for Turner, who was going to display an incredible knack for scouting other talent. Ike also worked as a session musician and production assistant for Sam Phillips and the Bihari Brothers, as well as supplying instruments to BB King's records, among others. Modern Records' Joe Bijari was so pleased with the fiery Turner that he hired him as a talent scout to identify other southern musicians worth recording in the North.

Turner also continued to write original material, albeit the Bihari Brothers were copyrighting his melodies under their own name without his knowledge because he was still green and naïve. Turner estimates that he may have penned 75 hit records for the Biharis and Modern.

Then there was his unique aptitude for spotting and fostering talent, which would come into its own over the next four years. Turner discovered or unearthed musicians such as Bobby Blue Bland, Howlin' Wolf, and Roscoe Gordon for Bihari, as well as playing piano with them on multiple sessions and on records by the soon-to-be-famous Little Milton. Turner discovered Little Junior Parker around this time, about 1952, and also played piano on his debut single, "You're My Angel/Bad Women, Bad Whiskey," starring Parker's Blue Flames.

Turner, ever the workaholic, continued to work for Phillips at Sun, for whom he cut two Wolf recordings, "How Many More Years" and "Moanin' at Midnight," which Phillips forwarded over to the legendary Chess Records label. Turner then surreptitiously took Wolf across the state line and re-recorded the tracks without the knowledge of Phillips or Chess, sending the results to Modern. Not content with only scouting talent, he attempted to steal Elmore James from Trumpet Records and record him for Modern as well.

Ike Turner ran his soon-reformed band the Kings of Rhythm like a cult, taking compulsive control over every idea and gesture of his band. Turner's discipline (a nicer word for compulsion) became famous, with his insistence on having the entire band live in one enormous house compound with him so he could conduct early morning practices. Turner, ironically, claimed to be a teetotaler at this point, eschewing all drugs and alcohol and insisting that all of his band members adopt the same "pure" lifestyle, fining anyone who breached his rigorous standards.

He reportedly penalized or even physically injured band members who played incorrect notes, and he had complete control over everything from their musical compositions to the matching clothes they wore on stage. This is the foresighted talent scout, control freak, and fanatical mentor who was going to meet one Anna Mae Bullock from Nutbush, the most extraordinary talent he had the good fortune to meet.

However, given her nostalgic memories of her sleepy childhood town, which she later expressed in her wistfully rocking "Nutbush City Limits," it's both ironic and telling that on the same album that featured that rural hymn to home, she also penned a completely contradictory song called "Fancy Annie." It's a gritty, raunchy stomper reminiscent of the Rolling Stones' "Brown Sugar" from their Sticky Fingers album, released two years before Tina's Nutbush City Limits.

Rather than merely opining about her little gospel-oriented community in this second song, she also celebrated that other St. Louis-oriented Tina we're about to meet, appearing to be conflicted by nature and being pushed in two separate and opposing directions.

"Fancy Annie was as sweet as candy, and she was never lonely because her joints were fantastic." But Annie forgot about the passage of time, and she lost her health and nearly her mind. Sure, Fancy Annie."

As a result, she had two competing origin myths: the tranquil country girl from Nutbush and the wild city girl from East St. Louis. She would constantly be in a constant state of conflict between the person she was and the person Ike wanted her to be.

CHAPTER 2:
PLEASE PASS ME THAT MICROPHONE

Sometimes the seemingly joyful accidents that help creative artists discover themselves and find their way ahead into their own careers are the most essential things that can happen to them. Perhaps, whether we recognize it or not, it is true of all of us in our lives. There are no happy or unhappy accidents for someone like Tina Turner, who believes in the notion of karma. Accidents happen, not twists and turns.

During rigorous investigation on a subject's trajectory, one can end up in some unexpected areas. It was my chance of finding the official record of Ike Turner's earlier attempts to showcase a main female performer inside his Kings of Rhythm outfit that sparked my interest. Several noteworthy entries for the summer of 1953 can be found in the Memphis Music Recording Service library and concealed in plain sight inside the archives of the Sun Records label. A decade before Ike hit gold with Tina, they were an odd blend of media release, public affairs announcement, and internal recorded memorandum.

"Jud Phillips joins Sun Records label to help with the increasing publicity activity to promote sales for Rufus Thomas / Chess Records issues recordings by Joseph Dobbins, made in Memphis this June / Sam Phillips makes his first recordings by a white group made for the Sun label, the Ripley Cotton Choppers / Elvis Presley pays $3.98 to record "My Happiness" at Memphis Recording Services."

The archive then lists a new studio session with Ike and "Bonnie" Turner after providing some context: "Following the success of 'Rocket 88' in 1951, Ike Turner spent much of the next three years helping to find and record various blues musicians across the south." Ike returned to Clarksdale in 1952 and was touring with his Kings of Rhythm band, and according to Eugene Fox, he traveled to Memphis somewhere in the summer of 1953, thus Ike's records with Bonnie are most likely from the same era, though you never know with Ike." Thus, the record demonstrates that even during his forays into the esoteric realm of talent scouting, he was still playing with his original band, and as early as 1952, he kind of stenciled the imprint for an early version of the Turner Revue format with the single "My Heart Belongs to You," backed by "Looking for My Baby," featuring the curious credits "Bonnie and Ike Turner" on vocals. But his voice, flat and thin, devoid of depth or emotion, indicated he was considerably more effective as a dominating if arrogant bandleader, yelling instructions to all and sundry.

According to the Sun collection, "due to his involvement in a slew of pre-Sun recordings, Ike Turner was frequently apportioned studio time for his own needs." As the itinerant leader of the Kings of Rhythm, he introduced into the ranks a coquettish piano player conveniently known as 'Bonnie Turner.'" She was described as "one of the less chronicled female acquaintances in Ike's life, she nevertheless showed little promise on the spirited song 'Love Is a Gamble.'"

The archive entry continues to praise her rapid delivery and her lovely but ultimately unremarkable voice. The results, however, were not considered publishable because she lacked both gravitas and power. The scouts at Sun couldn't tell if she was truly playing the piano. Bonnie's vocals were simply not that excellent, and based on the facts, she was thought unlikely to ever create a career around them.

Her only advantage, it seemed, was that she could appear to play the piano well enough for Ike to give up his stool and focus on his new Fender Stratocaster; in fact, as the record shows, it may have been her piano playing that allowed him to browse the shiny new guitars of Houck's music store in Memphis in the first place. That's some good payola.

The Sun Records collection also contains an unusual photograph of Ike and his Kings performing at the Birdcage club in 1955, with the credits identifying "singer and pianist Annie Mae Wilson," Bonnie's next vocal replacement in the Kings. He wanted to have his reserves stocked, and Ike seemed to collect Anna Maes as well as spouses. It's no surprise that Turner's story is winding.

Sun's library includes other, comparable rough pans of Annie Mae Wilson, Bonnie's replacement, who was also deemed less than great. The verdicts had to have been disheartening for the ladies and would have been discouraging for anyone but Ike Turner, who appeared to have a regular stream of damsels whom he might perhaps mold into gold.

In fact, in 1969, with Bonnie and Anna Mae Wilson long gone and Tina fronting the band, Ike revisited his song "Rock Me Baby" for their Outta Season LP, establishing that Ike's approach to the song hadn't changed much in sixteen years, but it also demonstrated how much he desperately needed Tina.

Many people have mistakenly identified Tina with two songs recorded by Ike at Sun Records in 1953 (unlikely given that she was still a fourteen-year-old singing in church choirs at the time), although it appears that "Bonnie" did the demos and Tina triumphantly went on to take her place in the band, even reprising the earlier version of "Rock Me Baby" but really rocking it this time.

The two songs "Old Brother Jack" and "Way Down in the Congo," recorded at Sun Studios on August 2, 1953 (but not released until 1976), are mentioned in Gerri Hirshey's book on soul music, Nowhere to Run, as reflections of "Tina's emotive early sessions." The author stated that "Turner had a girlfriend, first known as Anna Mae Bullock, then as Bonnie Turner, and now as Tina."

According to Hirshey's conflation of the three singers (a Bonnie and two Annas), Tina's entire surrender to Ike may be heard on her first recordings. "There is no connection between the microphone-swallowing Acid Queen and the timorous child singing 'Old Brother Jack' and 'Way Down in the Congo,' recorded in 1953." The voice has all the confidence of a starving child singing for its meal." The author is partially true, as there is nothing to connect Bonnie Turner's childhood voice with Tina Turner's mature voice, but only because they are the distinctively different voices of two completely different individuals.

Bonnie was Ike's first attempt at building a Revue framework, over a decade before Tina arrived on his scene, but with a vocalist who wasn't nearly as strong as the one who propelled him to the top of the charts later on. In the interim, he'd try another ill-fated female partnership, this time with another Annie Mae (Miss Wilson). It's no surprise that historians have been perplexed by Ike's liaisons. But it was his third attempt, Tina, that turned out to be the golden egg. He was also certain that he would soon meet the appropriate type of rocking lady who was gorgeous enough to keep up with him and his band.

As the founder of Sun Records observed, he couldn't do the singing himself. The famous black and white record pioneer Sam Phillips recalled both Ike's skills and his liabilities for a Miami Herald story by Rod Harmon ("Ike Turner's Star Is Rising, Despite Scars of Infamy"): "I listened to Ike sing and told him in no uncertain terms I just didn't see him as a singer." The inflections, the phrase, none of it was there. But he was a whale of a damn musician, one of the best piano players I'd heard up to that point, he just needed someone else to do the singing." From the start of his career, he would rely on someone else to deliver the vocals, going from person to person to find the right one.

Hirshey also related an experience she had with Tina at a Long Island dinner theater (before her comeback) in which she stated the singer wasn't keen on talking about the Memphis days while she was writing her otherwise highly read account of the soul sound, Nowhere to Run (1984). But it wasn't her who was in Memphis; it was Bonnie and Annie. The singer's admission into a Buddhist group famed for its delicate chanting, so different from the dry screech she's recognized for, did strike me as valuable in their dialogue. "She claims her current success is a payoff for a mother lode of bad karma: there's no other explanation for the first half of her life being so bad." She doesn't believe in coincidences. Although their marriage may have appeared to be a slow-motion disaster on the highway, Ike was no accident."

But it was "Bonnie Turner" (legally Marion Louise "Bonnie"), who had traveled much earlier on that treacherous road, with whom Ike recorded and published a few jumpy rhythm-and-blues singles, such as "Lookin' for My Baby" in 1952, and this Bonnie who was there at Sun Studios in 1953. I've even seen newspaper photos of Bonnie Turner with a credit line that says "AKA Tina." The confusion is understandable, given Ike's erratic behavior. Turner was married at least ten (or twelve) times, and he frequently claimed to have been married fifteen times, once to a fifteen-year-old girl.

His first marriage was to Edna Dean Stewart, who died of a heroin overdose when he was still in his teens. He later married Rosa Lee Sane, a woman with apparent mental disorders who was committed to an asylum by her family. He married Bonnie Mae Wilson, a member of the Kings of Rhythm, in 1953, but she left him after two years for another guy. Following that, he briefly married "Alice from Arkansas," and he later became associated with the previously mentioned Annie Mae Wilson, his second unsuccessful vocal protégée, who left him for a police officer. He then married Lorraine Taylor and had two boys with her.

By 1956, Ike had acquired another singer, this time a guy named Billy Gayle, who sang on a minor hit with Federal called "I'm Tore Up," but Gayle would also soon leave, cementing another aggravating behavior pattern. For reasons that will become clear as history progresses, not many individuals enjoyed being around Ike Turner. His multifarious abilities were eclipsed by his already notorious rage and brutality. "He had a very, very bad reputation," Tina subsequently told Vanity Fair magazine. "He was already known as the 'pistol-whipping Turner.'"

Long after his romance with Tina ended, he married a former Ikette, Margaret Ann Thomas, in 1981, indicating that he was not yet married. After his final release from prison, he was met at the iron gates by another Ikette, blues musician Jeanette Bazzell, who married him in 1995. Finally, in 2006, he married his "music collaborator" at the time, Audrey Madison, who divorced him shortly before his death in 2007.

The day he died, Thomas, with whom he had restored a connection, discovered him unconscious at his house. He appears to have enjoyed getting married; he definitely did not enjoy being married, but he did enjoy getting married. Sometimes I suppose a coroner could have appropriately classified the cause of death as twofold: Ike Turner and marriage.

In some ways, he was a modern-day Bill Cosby predator figure, but without the use of quaaludes or other poisonous medications to get his way with women. Despite his shortcomings, Ike's only seduction ingredient was the overpowering force of his own captivating personality: Ike was both the drug he provided and the poisonous material.

And in the spirit of both momentous karma and unintentional coincidence, the initial encounter between sixteen-year-old Anna Mae Bullock and twenty-five-year-old Ike Turner would prove both providential and perplexing. By 1956, he was already regarded as something of a music industry icon, but their combined tale—and subsequently her own career—was only just getting started. All it took was Anna Mae's passionate remark that the singer and his band had "put her in a trance." Little did she know, she was merely the next in a long line of starry-eyed young girls who had been equally fascinated by Ike.

When it came to playing kids' games in the country with her older sister Alline, Anna Mae normally followed her lead, and as she grew into adult girlhood, she also followed her lead right into the dens of inequality that studded a lively city like St. Louis. All of the intriguing new adult games were taking place there.

Remember, the two country-girl sisters learned all about music from two limited and drastically disparate sources: the gospel sounds of sanctified church gatherings (which could get plenty raucous and kick up quite a ruckus, including much frenzied dancing) and the tiny tinny radio they listened to while cooking up sliced potatoes on the top of their family's old kitchen stove. The sounds they heard sweeping throughout the country in the mid-1950s were enough to make any kid's blood pumping quicker, and the Bullock sisters were no exception, albeit more removed from the urban din at the time. They were, however, well prepared to rock and roll.

Anna Mae also liked to incorporate some of the twangy energy she heard on their father's wooden radio into her own personal fantasy plays, which she performed at her mother's bedroom dressing table when she thought no one was looking (though her mother later commented on her boisterous little performances with disdainful amusement). This girl appeared to be a natural performer from the start.

She'd draw the two side mirrors together, enclosing her petite figure, and pretend to play piano by hammering on the counter top with unrestrained abandon, accepting the acclaim of the phantom crowds with elegant bows. This motif would subsequently explode into the genuine yells of massive adoring crowds in stadium-scale shows as she began her radical change into Tina.

In fact, if it's correct to claim Ike as the inventor of a new hybrid of boogie, blues, and rockabilly that became known as rock and roll (which I tend to believe because it took Little Richard six years to lift the opening bars of "Rocket 88" and launch a revolution alongside Chuck Berry's similarly lifted guitar solos, himself a mix of Ike Turner and the incredible Sister Rosetta Tharpe), then Tina Turner was almost.

I've always been perplexed when people associate or discuss Tina in the same soul music context as, say, James Brown, Aretha Franklin, or Sharon Jones. She was never, ever, really a soul singer to me, despite the fact that her bluesy style of sensual rocking and rolling was soulful for sure, and she did deliver the occasional soul-based song brilliantly.

Despite many differences in her developing approaches throughout the years, Aaron Cohen believes Tina Turner was essentially a soul music artist, but one who expanded the bounds of what that might imply. "I believe so," he told me, "but my definition of soul music' is perhaps more broad than most others'." But I would categorize her as a soul singer in any case: coming out of gospel, bringing that type of singing to black secular music, the call-and-response between her and her band, all of that is what anyone would consider soul, or at the very least R&B. Anyway, what is soul if Tina Turner performing 'Knock on Wood' in the late 1960s?" I perceive a rhetorical question there, which is understandable.

Of course, Ike was the polar antithesis of soul music. He didn't have a soul bone in his skinny body: boogie blues and almost a jitterbug vibe till Tina pushed him in a whole different way. Anne Mae's journey to self-expression and emancipation, with a dash of perdition thrown in for good measure, began with that old wooden radio on the stove. Things "started getting crazy" for her in the middle of 1956, a year when all of America seemed to be in the grip of the new kind of music: rhythm and blues mingled with rockabilly and country, the exotic amalgam of black and white emotive sound structures primarily or most publicly introduced by Bill Haley and the Comets and, soon enough, the earth-shattering arrival of Elvis.

After jazz, rock & roll was unquestionably one of the first truly urban music styles. If you're from Nutbush, an unorganized tiny town with no city lines, any city seems large. St. Louis proper, albeit enormous in comparison to Nutbush, was a rather peaceful area in the mid-1950s for Anna Mae. But East St. Louis was something else entirely. That was where the action was, especially Alline's brand of naughty action, and it never seemed to stop—cat houses, gambling dens, countless music clubs and pubs, roadhouses, juke joints, and a never-ending nightlife that lasted all day and night.

There were tantalizing temptations for a young, rather small, and wide-eyed country girl with an older sister she looked up to who could guide her through the stunning bright lights of the Blue Note,

Birdcage, Sportsman, Lakeside, Perry's Lounge, Kingsbury's Lounge, Garrett's Lounge, and others, sometimes on the same night. It was a new way of living, with a lot of lounging going on. Many of these joints (that's the only word for them) didn't even require keys to lock up because they were open 24 hours a day, 365 days a year. Who needs vacations when life is already a vacation?

East St. Louis provided ways and means for artists (a peculiar species to begin with) to be what could only be described as absurdly joyful. And in the center of it all, like a reigning monarch, was lanky and languid Ike Turner, the leader of an exciting rhythm trio that Alline couldn't stop gushing over. Anna Mae, who was only sixteen at the time, was awestruck by her sister, who was already frequenting clubs and dating scary dudes who picked her up in large Cadillacs and Lincolns. One of them, Leroy Tyus, owned the Tail of the Cock, where Alline worked as a barmaid, but she was widely known throughout town.

After her different male dates, she and her girlfriends would go to watch Ike Turner perform at Club D'Lisa (you didn't bring boyfriends to see Ike since they wouldn't like him, and he definitely didn't like them), and then after hours, from 2:00 a.m. Until the end of time, he would sit on Manhattan's throne-like stage, directing the activity in the room as if he were shooting a Fellini film, which, in some bizarre way, he was. Anna Mae considered it to be the ultimate jumping joint, almost as if every small hole-in-the-wall club down south had been smashed together into one circus-like arena up north, dressed up in her sister's clothes and dolled up with makeup to look older and more serious than she really was.

It must have felt like Las Vegas when Elvis was there, otherworldly, heady beyond description, especially to this young rural girl pretending to be a more urban adult, with 250 seats for squirming patrons (yes, mostly women) waiting for Ike to strut his stuff from the stage set up in the center of the room with tables encircling it and a gigantic painting of the Kings of Rhythm hanging up on the wall. When Alline and Anna Mae arrived, the band would already be performing, as was their usual before King Ike appeared.

And when he did, you could feel it, Anna Mae later recalled Kurt Loder. "He had David Bowie's body back then—great." His suit appeared to be hung on a hanger. "What an immaculate-looking black man," she thought, but even at her tender age, she knew he wasn't her type. For one thing, his teeth and haircut were all incorrect, looking like a wig had been put on, and on closer inspection, she could see that he was plain ugly in her opinion. But there was something else about him. "He then got up onstage and took up his guitar." He only hit one note. And the joint began to rock."

The dance floor was packed with sweaty people gyrating, and Anna Mae was perplexed as to why so many women liked him considering what she thought he looked like. But she kept staring at him while listening to his incredibly tight band, which was as sonically bonded together as only a band that has played a song 10,000 times could be. She was enthralled, as has been widely reported. She and the other couple of hundred swaying dames and ladies were astonished by his charisma and waiting for an opportunity to catch his eye—exactly how King Ike wanted his kingdom to roll.

In an unusual manner, she was hooked right away. It wasn't love at first sight, by any means; it was more like awe. It felt inevitable that she would be up on that stage, singing out in the midst of all those whirling lights and twisting bodies, sooner or later. It took a bit, as the inevitable often does, but it was inevitable, she thought, and her sister was plainly the way to hasten it.

In yet another sequence of seeming karmic influences (as Tina Turner would later doubtless feel given her increasing philosophical and spiritual inclinations), sister Alline had been dating, among her numerous beaus, Eugene Washington, drummer for the Kings of Rhythm. Over the next several weeks, Gene began to notice that his girlfriend was often showing up with her younger sister, who was still a gangly junior at Summer High School. Washington, who felt the girl's vibes like electricity but also understood Ike's tastes in girls (usually big and round, all around), thought she was far too underweight and underfed by country standards to ever really pique his majesty's interest.

But the former rhythm man and longtime Ike cult member was smart enough to know that he needed to cultivate Alline's mother's friendship and gain her trust and affection (today I believe we refer to this cultivation process as grooming)—or perhaps I should say, as a skilled enabler, he was devious enough to do so. He actually asked her mother, whom he had grown to know slightly, if Anna Mae could go to Manhattan as long as he looked after her (which, when you think about it, is like enlisting the protection of a crocodile). And Anna's mother, who was never known for her maternal instincts, agreed.

Washington, the drummer, had a platform erected above the rest of the band from which he could view the young fan and her restless need to sing along. He even dangled a microphone off the edge of the platform to pick up on the chirps and warbles of one of the most excited audience members. Anna Mae became a regular at most of the venues where King Ike was performing and established a connection with the band's bassist, Jessie Knight, among others, in what appeared to be a deliberate attempt to penetrate Turner's realm.

She even persuaded her sister Alline to ask Eugene Washington to ask Ike if she could try a song sometime, which he mumbled some lukewarm approval to but never really followed up on because she was not his type of dame (even Anna Mae was positive). Eventually, her patience ran out, and during an intermission one night—during a quiet spell when most of the band was hanging out, smoking or drinking, but Ike was up alone onstage playing the organ by himself—Anna Mae recognized the song he was tinkering with, a BB King song called "You Know I Love You."

Washington emerged from outside, now half plastered, and proceeded to playfully give the microphone to his girlfriend Alline, who, despite being a very dangerous party girl, would never be caught dead singing in public. Observers can recall what happened next, and Anna Mae will never forget it because it was the moment fate stood up and yelled, "You!" She took the mic and began singing along, "I love you for myself but you're gone and left me for someone else, when night began to fall I cry alone...", prompting Ike to pull up short, jump offstage with a wailing "Girl!," pick her up off her feet, and demand to know what else she could sing. Anna Mae's reaction was as straightforward as it was honest when she gently stated, "Well, everything they play on the radio, I guess."

Knowing the Anna Mae we all know today, it's difficult to fathom a teenager, someone who had never sang professionally, wanting to jump onstage with this strange but fascinating guy who had been there for years. But knowing the latter Tina, we can imagine her audacity in believing, as described by Maureen Orth in a Vanity Fair interview, "Of course, I was very excited." I'm also quite competent because I've been a vocalist my entire life." That's all sixteen years of it.

Turner was completely taken aback by the harsh voice emanating from this skinny kid, whom he had already deceptively nicknamed Little Ann. Orth also mentioned Ike's tactic of utilizing self-pity to win compassion from the obvious raw talent in front of him. "My issue is that people always take my songs away from me, and my singers always abandon me." He was so taken by her voice and enthusiasm that he couldn't believe she was only a teenager with the voice of an old Bessie Smith howler. "When I got there," Tina told Orth, "Ike was so shocked, and he never let me go."

So Ike played some songs she recognized, and the band started to join in as she performed "Since I Fell for You" and a duet with Jimmy Thomas on "Love Is Strange." It certainly is. Her mother, Zelma, was none too pleased when she realized that her daughter was already singing semi-regularly instead of doing what she expected her to do: being a nurse or a maid. Surprisingly, Anna Mae would be a nurse and a maid in a few short years, but with only one patient: Ike.

To Zelma's horror, he sent his second failed effort at a vocalist, Anna Mae Wilson, over looking for his new young discovery. After that, he sent his devoted drummer to pose as a chaperone because, like all characters of his ilk, he needed to befriend the girl's mother in order to have complete and easy access to the girl (at this point, merely to her voice). He then went over to see her mother in person and charmed her, as he was able to do with most people, vowing to personally take care of her and make sure nothing horrible ever happened.

According to Off the Record, her voice was truly outstanding, and perhaps even worth conspiring over. "When I first started singing with Ike, I was basically modeling myself after the majority of the male singers I was exposed to, such as Ray Charles and Sam Cooke." My mother's and sister's voices, I believe, are likewise heavy. I believe the raspiness is a natural sound. But it was my environment that inspired my style. Pretty singing is not my thing; I want them to be harsh."

Despite the weird maturity of her voice, she was so young when she started that she didn't truly see what was going on in the dynamics of their budding relationship. She even stated to everyone that Ike was extremely wonderful to her when she first started her career, even going so far as to claim that because she was still in high school and only sang on weekends, they became close friends and lived what she believed was a fun life.

She also felt sad for his sob story, which I'm sure he was depending on, and she could even empathize with him (her inherent skill), which I'm sure he meticulously planned and amplified. "He was broken hearted because every time he got a hit record on somebody, of course they got to be the star," she told Gerri Hirshey in a GQ magazine article. "The man was very nice to me, and way before our relationship really started, I promised him that I wouldn't leave him." Her statement was almost prophetic in nature.

Their relationship was initially sibling-like, in a foreboding sort of way, but Ike wasted no time, partly because he was a brilliant talent scout, partly because he was a jerk, and entirely because he suddenly saw and heard what his previous protégées Bonnie and Annie Mae Wilson were missing. Turner went on a shopping binge and purchased new stage clothing. He dressed her in what appeared to be a female impersonator costume: extremely high stiletto heels, nylons, and skintight, clingy, sequin miniskirts. That's when I believe he felt the future approaching and jumped on board.

No doubt the other Club Manhattan patrons, especially the women who had an unfathomable fascination with Ike, looked down on this small girl as she suddenly assumed a regular role onstage. Perhaps disdain is a mild word for it; it was pure contempt for someone they felt was simply cashing in her meal ticket. However, this could not be further from the truth.

Anna Mae was simply drinking up the exciting glitter and reveling in the attention lavished on her for what she always felt was an intrinsic vocal talent, and it was King Ike who spotted his one-way ticket away from the dives of St. Louis. He fantasized of reaching the respectable theaters and concert halls he so desired, such as the Regal Theater in Chicago, the Howard Theater in Washington, or the Apollo Theater in New York, the holy grail of all music performance cathedrals.

He was crazy, but he was almost always correct, and the other members of his Rhythm Kings knew it when they heard it in Anna Mae: something out of this world, a magical sound element you can't just make no matter how skilled a musician you are. Loder put it succinctly: "Her voice combined the emotional force of the great blues singers with a sheer, wallpaper-peeling power that seemed made to order for the age of amplification." She was also about to inadvertently invent rock music, in my opinion.
Drummer Eugene Washington couldn't believe his ears either, noting that women don't usually get away with this much raw power, unless they're Bessie Smith, and he was well aware that up until that point, he, Ike, and the other Kings had been delivering solid but simple and down-home boogie-swing numbers. This was a whole new ballgame, and it was the real deal, an original style, not simply covers of other people's songs. Ike could now pen it, and Anna Mae could deliver it. It was a marriage made in heaven.

Their first appearance as Ike and Tina Turner was as the opening act for a BB King concert on January 9, 1956, at the Café Royale in Lake Charles, Louisiana, after he mistakenly "discovered" her future singing fame. A vintage poster depicts King singing his song "Every

Day I Have the Blues" with special "guest" (singular) Ike and Tina Turner, the newly minted Tina still just seventeen years old.

At this point, another member of Ike's squad, Raymond Hill from his "Rocket 88" days, was serving as her first official "boyfriend." They moved in together, and he stayed for a while before leaving, cordial but perhaps not fiery enough to match "Little Ann," as Anna Mae was still known privately at the time. Ike stepped in, and despite having gotten his other girlfriend pregnant, he became really platonic with Anna Mae to the extent where when she became pregnant, Ike's girlfriend Lorraine assumed it was Ike's. She was well aware of Ike's penchant for getting women pregnant.

Even though Anna Mae was pregnant with Raymond Hill's baby, not Ike's, her struggle with Ike's jealous girlfriend was heightened. On August 20, 1958, eighteen-year-old Anna Mae gave birth to Hill's son Craig (who sadly committed suicide in 2018), while on October 3, Ike's girlfriend Lorraine gave birth to hers: Ike Jr. This was clearly a freight train going at breakneck speed, bound for who knows where. But I believe Ike and Anna Mae both knew exactly what they wanted from the other and what they were going to receive out of the deal—to a point. By this point, Raymond Hill had passed her by, so Anna Mae briefly worked as a nurse's aide in Barnes Hospital's maternity ward to make ends meet.

Ike, as usual, was fighting tooth and nail with his band mates, the singers (particularly Lorraine), and anybody else who got in his way. The next thing she knew, "Little Ann" was officially named lead vocalist of the group, so she dutifully moved back out of her mother's house (not liking it much with her anyhow) and into Ike's house and East St. Louis cultish artists commune. An unpleasant note was already lingering in the air. That was the first time Anna Mae realized Ike Turner was going to play a significant role in her life.

It must have felt like she was the still-adolescent star of her own film, but it was real life. She subsequently described it as, without really realizing it at the time, Ike moving in on her life—a strange choice of words that couldn't possibly augur well for everybody involved. To commemorate the event, he increased her weekly compensation to a whopping $25. To make it fully official, he'd have to transform her into Tina Turner. That's exactly what he did.

CHAPTER 3:
ROYALTY IN CHITLIN'

Blues, jazz, rock and roll, soul, and funk all arose from the transformation of struggle into creativity. The Chitlin' Circuit was a network of performance venues throughout America's southern, eastern, and upper Midwest regions that provided commercial and cultural acceptance for African American musicians and other artists during the era of racial segregation. The name is a joke on the Borscht Belt, a resort area popular with Jewish artists in the 1940s and 1960s. It is derived from the soul food item chitterlings (stewed pig intestines). The live performance touring club circuit employed hundreds of black musicians and eventually resulted in the creation of rock and roll as an unintended side effect.

Music is also frequently inextricably linked to big social issues, as Aaron Cohen emphasized in Move On Up. "A generation born at the tail end of the African American Great Migration struggled with segregation, integration, and deindustrialization." "Music ran alongside civil rights activism, and some performers contributed to that crusade." Tina Turner was unquestionably one of the most important of all.

The circuit word, paradoxically, memorializes the cultural past of black people, who were frequently given only the intestines of the pig to eat rather than bacon or ham, thus coming to symbolize developing a taste out of necessity but eventually liking and identifying with it. Within this ostensibly lowly entertainment context, Ike and Tina Turner came to embody a certain type of majesty, which helped elevate it into a cultural phenomenon. Their Revue would provide one of the first significant possibilities for big white audiences to absorb black musical motifs. They were also the busiest entertainers on the planet at the time.

In this regard, Aaron Cohen's comments to me on the interconnected nature of geographical and cultural effects are instructive. "The vast African American migration from north to south, as well as the music that resulted, is indeed too vast to adequately describe." From the 1940s to the 1960s, however, it was frequently bidirectional, with urban northern performers and musicians influencing Southern artists as much as Southerners bringing their sounds north (musicians going back and forth, producers and arrangers from Detroit working in Memphis and vice versa).

"What's intriguing about Tina Turner is that she appeared to be more global than exclusively American." I'm not sure if her eclecticism comes through in her embracing of Buddhism. Perhaps this international personal vision suited her well enough for her to have a plethora of inner resources to draw from when she staged her massive comeback later in the 1980s."

As Cohen clarified to me, the touring circuit was a powerful but also dangerous environment for performers: "While this may be a broad statement, I always understood the 'chitlin' circuit' to be the loosely (very loosely) organized network of performance venues for African American audiences that sprung up during segregation and, to a limited extent, still exist today." The circuit itself was packed with criminals and thugs (of all hues), and I've heard that Ike Turner was skilled at not just dealing with these guys violently, but also ensuring that his entire band was paid. I'm not sure whether that's accurate, but I can understand Tina Turner seeing him as a guardian in this situation, at least at first."

The astounding growth and evolution of musical forms linked to geographical shifts is a potent one for Toronto-based music writer and author John Corcelli. Corcelli agrees that these North-South artistic "trade routes" are vital in building a uniquely Yankee musical sense. "When it came to race relations in America, Turner had to forge her own artistic path." Unfortunately, many of the best American black singers had to play 'politically correct' events. That said, a gig is a gig, and if you chose to make your living through concert performances, you're no worse for wear.

"To me, Turner paid her musical dues by rigorously playing the 'chitlin circuit,' and she emerged from it as a kind of rite of passage, as so many other black performers had done before her." My key remark about that massive cultural migration is that it is responsible for our entire knowledge of contemporary American music. As the great Duke Ellington famously stated, "all American music is rooted in dreams."

James Porter, a keen observer of black rock music, believes that African American talent transcends geography and is well beyond the realm of either northern or southern sensibilities. The dream of freedom, whether political or artistic, knows no bounds. "That means one thing to me: limitless cultural aspiration." You are not limited to a single concept of darkness. You can redefine the medium as you see fit without anyone telling you it's not dark enough. Or at least white enough. This, I believe, was a result of African-American cultural migration—mentally, musically, and physically. The disadvantage of this is that some of the grittier southern sounds, such as blues, were left behind due to the mistaken notion that they were connected with hard times. Nonetheless, there remained vestiges of the blues in every mainstream black music until the disco era."

Despite their tight working and living relationship, I remain certain today of something I've long suspected: Ike Turner never had any love interest in Anna Mae Bullock. Perhaps conquest, but only in the broadest meaning of the word. I don't think he considered her attractive in the conventional sense, but he did have a profound and instantaneous realization that she was a genius, most likely because he was (or used to be). He needed her to realize his long-held fantasy of dominating the music industry, despite the fact that he was a little thinker who probably only wanted more club dates, a few more album sales, and more expensive drugs.

Meanwhile, as the 1950s came to an end, Ike was passing through other new singers like loaves of bread, striving for the correct formula, always deploying the Kings of Rhythm with interchangeable vocalists. On "You Keep Worrying Me," he attempted Brenston (the voice from "Rocket 88") again, Tommy Hodge on "I'm Gonna Forget About You," Betty Everett on "Tell Me Darling," and lastly he tried employing his new protégée, Anna Mae Bullock, primarily in the background, on their next throwaway single tune.

The first time her dry, breathy voice was heard on a recording, while still doing scenery, was in the novelty song "Box Top" in 1958, released to a silent response by a small local St. Louis label, Tune Town, and while still listed on the single as "Little Ann." It was an inauspicious beginning by the standards of what followed, but everyone has to start somewhere. Furthermore, what followed occurred very instantly and with a force and fury that equaled, if not outnumbered, the oncoming British invasion in pure intensity if not numbers.

Never one to shy away from further complicating his life, he'd separated with his fiancée Lorraine by 1959 and begun doing more of what he'd sworn Zelma he'd never do with her star-struck daughter. Anna Mae wasn't happy; she despised his open philandering, but she was stuck. Her greatest error was when it became more personal, and had it not become intimate and later aggressive, they might still be together. One thing she was certain of was that she was addicted to something, but it wasn't Ike; it was performing live music that she craved so intensely that she was ready to put up with Ike for a long time.

However, near the end of 1960, Anna Mae did become pregnant, this time clearly with Ike's child, and as if on cue, Lorraine returned to the scenario, causing Anna Mae to leave Ike and his Virginia Place home once more and take a little house back in St. Louis proper, where she hired a woman to look after her first son, Craig (Raymond Hill's), while she went to work. Even though she was pregnant, Anna Mae completed Ike's normal dizzying round of frenetic club engagements as well as live performances on select college campuses.

She gave birth to her second child, Ike's son Ronald, on October 27, but Ike insisted on her leaving the hospital just days later to perform with him in Oakland, California. She had to stay in the hospital according to doctor's instructions, so Ike hired an impersonator (who turned out to be a hooker) to resemble Tina. Tina would be dogged by the pop conspiracy rumor that she was, in reality, a prostitute for the rest of her life.

Anna Mae was no longer just the featured occasional singer in his band by this point; she was the full-time star vocalist. This was the period in which Ike was restlessly trying to replicate his early success nine years earlier, repetitively copying the same weary formula over and over, never seeming to comprehend that if he wanted a fresh hit album, he might try striking out in a new direction. When Anna Mae appeared at the edge of his stage, Ike recognized an opportunity to do what he'd been attempting to achieve with other female singers for the past decade or so. He simply related to her in the only way he knew how once he began to coordinate his career-making drive. He didn't appear to know any better, or he couldn't help himself, as he couldn't sustain a totally platonic business or creative relationship. After all, his view of male-female relationships was quite restricted and thuggish to say the least: have sex with them, marry them, make them pregnant, and hit them, in that order.

She was already in the early phases of becoming someone else at the time, living with Ike (and Lorraine) almost as if they were her adult chaperones. But, eventually, Ike split up with Lorraine and with Little Ann, who still thought he was looking out for her best interests (like a brother and sister, was her innocent assumption). Despite the fact that physical contact with him revolted her, Little Ann still innocently but sincerely believed she was in love (or a sort of love) with him, and she succumbed primarily because of everything she thought he was doing to aid her in her life and music career.

In addition to the frantic touring, she also took part in the second unavoidability, a new Ike song single, unfortunately titled "A Fool in Love," which was being recorded on the spot. It was a surprising hit the second time around. Ike had given the cassettes to some of his St. Louis deejay pals, who shared them with Henry "Juggy" Murray of Sue Records, one of the few record labels owned and operated by a black entrepreneur. Murray was immediately smitten by Little Ann's voice. He described himself as "smitten with the kitten."

The label owner flew to East St. Louis, ostensibly to meet Ike, where he encountered him in his regular realm of Cadillacs and young (typically white) girls. But it was Anna Mae he really wanted to meet, and he did, then stunned Ike by putting down a contract with a

$25,000 advance on the table and declaring that Ike should forgo his initial intention of rerecording the track with a male vocal. "It was really only Anna Mae who made the song work the way it did," he declared.

Even though Ike had been rejected by other labels before Sue Records, the record promoter supposedly knew from the first moment he heard the tape that it was going to be a hit. Ike was perplexed by Juggy's assurance, but he was undoubtedly intrigued and a bit awed by his assertiveness. He pondered why this new guy on the scene was so invested in a song that no one else was interested in, to which Juggy replied that they didn't know what he knew. In Loder's Turner testimonial, he is also believed to have stated that "Ike was a musical genius, but he wouldn't know a hit record if it fell off the Empire State Building and hit him on the head."

Murray was also the one who advised (always one to trust his instincts) that Ike really considered making Anna Mae the permanent up-front lead singer of his show, rather than just a support singer, because she was far too talented for that secondary role. That was what Ike had been wanting to hear for approximately ten years, and he announced, just like Juggy, that the new song will be released with Anna Mae as the main vocalist. But, even more opportunistically, he announced the birth (in his imagination, at that same moment) of a brand new group name to replace the Kings of Rhythm persona he'd been working with for so long.

Ike and Tina Turner would be credited with the new tune. This came as a major surprise to Anna Mae Bullock, who was unsure about taking on a stage name he'd made up in honor of a white blond television heroine named Sheena (of the Jungle) who he grew up fantasizing about. She was even more unsure about how deeply she was getting involved with a guy she didn't even like (while convincing herself that she loved him to get by) and despite the fact that she had lately had Ike's progeny living inside of her body.

Nonetheless, she remained intrigued by what she, a nobody little country girl, had accomplished as a result of his imposing presence in her life as a show business mentor and manager. His stated aim of moving to California, where he said the action was, if the new record was a hit, was especially striking, something that both appealed to and daunted her.

Her first encounters with what one might call the real Ike, the one hidden beneath his disguise of slick suits and magical rhythms, came not long into the rapidly accelerating arc of their performing career, including his plan to pay her rent expenses but keep all the money they made for himself (a decision that even a still youngish neophyte knew couldn't possibly be correct or fair). First, she objected to her name being changed. She had tried to explain that she didn't like the arrangement, that it was unjust, and that she didn't want anything to do with him in the first place. "Click" was a hidden button in his skull.

A danger switch went off, most likely related to his dream of making his third female lead singer in a row the one who made him rich, and he suddenly beat her up for the first time, using a shoe stretcher (later on, shoes themselves would be preferred method of pounding on her), leaving her with a swollen eye and the terrifying realization that her life had taken a sinister turn.

Of course, the nasty and even heinous side of their story has been fully documented in the 1993 film What's Love Got to Do with It?Following the singer's well-documented and widely publicized personal testimonial in 1986, the film has a grippingly dramatic Laurence Fishburne and Angela Bassett performance. These components were understandably expected to be contentious, and they were, with Ike loudly decrying his unfair treatment for two decades among a slew of lies and Tina steadfastly sticking to her side of the tale. He went to his grave, like most abusers, in denial about his own toxic behavior, preferring to blame everyone else.

The salient question from our vantage point now (and back then, as I recall) was this: which person in such a dynamic would one expect to have a firmer grasp on their memory and thus the accuracy of the narrative, the one who was blotted out on cocaine and ego rage, or the victim, who was repeatedly brutalized in a coercive lifestyle? I'd say the discussion is over. "Living with Ike was a high wire act, he'd jump on anything, just to fight," Tina wrote longingly in My Love Story. I had to tread lightly. In a strange sense, the bruises he inflicted on me were a symbol of ownership, another way of saying—she's mine, and I can do whatever I want with her. I knew it was time to go, but I didn't know where to begin."

It's just another chance for us to focus on two things that don't matter more but are just as important: first, how his warped genius as an impresario-producer brought her into our collective experience, and second, the singer's contribution to pop music history during her duet persona, particularly what she accomplished as a solo artist in her post-hostage phase. When dealing with a topic who was willing to go through enormous emotional hardships in order to publicly express herself creatively, it's always the music that counts the most to us because it's plainly what she cared about.

But, like many women, she first convinced herself that she had done something wrong, that she didn't fully appreciate him, that she didn't want to leave him just as his business was taking off, and that she could work harder to make things better between them—a usual list of justifications. The important thing she was ignoring in her personal rationalization technique was that it was she, not him, who was the secret to his success, just as the eccentric Juggy Murray had foretold. Thank god for Juggy's subtle convincing that Anna Mae is the true star.

Following their first hit, "A Fool in Love," and with truly blazing ambition, Ike decided the time had come to do two things: expand their touring schedule while simultaneously returning to the studio. The important thing to remember about Ike and Tina at this point is that her future husband and manager were operating under the assumption that his dream was coming true, but that it could all end quickly, so he had to perform, write, and record as if there was no tomorrow just in case there wasn't.

A regular stream of songs, especially singles, tumbled out of his mind like leaves from a tree someplace in the back of his busy mind. In total, they released sixty-eight singles, twenty-seven LP albums, twenty compilation records, and twelve live LP albums during their tenure together. Some were obviously better than others, but they were all interesting and captivating to some extent, especially if they predominantly showcased the torchy gifts of his young new girlfriend from down south.

The group's second record, ominously named "I Idolize You," reached number 5 on the R&B charts and number 82 on the Billboard mainstream charts in December 1960. Sue Records released their debut album, The Soul of Ike and Tina Turner (although I'm not sure if it was genuinely soul music), in 1961, with a slew of rapidly successful songs, including the equally ironically titled "It's Gonna Work Out Fine."

According to James Porter, it was the intrinsic tendency of rhythm and blues to erupt into rock merely by expressing its essential ideals at a higher level. "When Ike and Tina initially started making noise as a couple, the line between rock and roll and rhythm and blues was blurred. Prior until around 1965, even the smoothest vocal groups were known as 'rock & roll,' even if modern ears could hear them as rhythm & blues. While Ike & Tina's early releases were very much in the R&B genre of the time, glimmers of 'rock & roll' would occasionally peek through. Witness, for example, the blazing guitar intro to 'It's Gonna Work Out Fine,' which precludes any easy classification, and with Ike and Tina, we can certainly witness powerful purveyors of the subliminal threshold between these two styles.

When discussing the details for Vanity Fair, Tina stated flatly that she would have loved to leave him at this stage, but "I was caught in his web." This was also the period during which he began regularly clobbering her out of nowhere, and if she dared to ask him what she had done wrong to provoke this bad treatment, he would pound on her even more.

In a subsequent GQ essay, she revealed that there was ongoing pressure to make more hit singles and recordings, and that even though she had made him famous, she was the innocent one being tortured. "I just went home, put on an ice pack, and sang for the next few days." I simply kept going."

Marriage has always been a means to an end for Ike. He enlisted Tina's help in safeguarding them from prior wives seeking shared income by just marrying his young new vocalist in order to control any money he had accumulated via her talents. Ike's insatiable desire for more hit songs seemed to be matched only by the public's want for more Tina tunes. In 1964, he published Get It on Cenco Records, as well as Her Man His Woman on Capitol Records.

He also went on a one-off spree, releasing Ike and Tina Turner Revue Live on Kent Records, Ike and Tina Live Volume 2 on Loma Records, and a second version with the same title on Warner Bros., the latter of which peaked at number 126 on the Billboard chart. That year would be their genuine recording borderline: a sort of holding pattern between their future wall-of-sound adventure with the similarly crazy producer Phil Spector. Ike would embrace that pinnacle as well, and even if it didn't truly involve his input, he could always claim credit for it.

Ike had gone into overdrive. Art Lassiter, Ike's frontman for the Kings of Rhythm, had already stolen Ray Charles's notion of a support group of pretty women to add some spice to his concerts, a trio he called the Artettes after Ray's fem format called the Raelettes. Guess what Ike named his own trio of hot women to back up his new singing wonder Tina after "A Fool in Love" began to fire up the charts. He naturally took the already stolen idea and christened them the Ikettes, never one to reinvent the wheel excessively, but rather to merely improve on its current design.

"A Fool in Love" was an outstanding debut, with raw and gritty pulsations, enormously thumping bass lines, and a sharply articulate tapping drumming cadence, all with Tina Turner yelping away to her heart's chagrin on top of the mix, exactly where she belonged. It was just some simple but lasting magic in it that appeared to come out of nowhere, and it still delivers a punch all these years after. A case of sui generis, ex nihilo, born from nothing, unique as a species that does not appear to fit into any other species.

It's like a blind date for Mahalia Jackson and James Brown, or a double date for Ray Charles and Rosetta Tharpe. It is one of Tina's most essential songs since, being her debut, it established the paradigm for everything that came after. On her very first featured vocalist stint, she had made it into Ike's first national hit, one of the first rhythm-and-blues tracks to cross to pop charts and go on to become a million seller, with a B-side of "The Way You Love Me" for dessert.

Of course, Ike's first hit had been incorrectly attributed to him a decade before, leaving him laboring mainly as a regional artist. There would be no mistake this time, with Tina fronting his band, and Rolling Stone would properly label it as one of the blackest records to ever slip into the Billboard Hot 100 since Ray Charles arrived.

The song just cooked, with Tina's blistering lead vocal, accompaniment by the Kings of Rhythm, and background vocals by Robbie Montgomery, Sandra Harding, and Frances Hodges, all while being led on the piano by its creator and producer, Ike Turner. This is also the song that would kick off their physically taxing tour of one-night circuit stands, including their first primal descent into the Apollo Theater, which resulted in the group's stunning performance on American Bandstand, much to the astonishment of a very young, conservatively dressed Dick Clark. It also had an impact on Tina, who continued to sing the song much later in her solo career, including during her final concert tour in 2000.

Tina was in the hospital with hepatitis contracted after making the record, which was complicated by a case of jaundice while convalescing, and she found herself staring at the ceiling in bewilderment as their new hit single played out on the hospital's radio that summer and fall. "He's got me smilin' when I should be ashamed, and he's got me laughin' when my heart is in pain."

Ike had her sneak out of the hospital at night, sending one of his henchmen to pick her up, and he forced her to make an improvised stage costume out of a baby-bump-concealing sack shape with loads of chiffon on top, hop into a station wagon, and be driven all the way to Cincinnati.

This was Ike and Tina Turner's debut live concert as a duo, now formally known as a Revue, with "A Fool in Love" reaching number two on the R&B charts. The tour gained as much traction as the song, bringing them to the Apollo Theater in New York on a massive star-studded bill featuring Hank Ballard and Lee Dorsey, as well as Tina, who was eight months pregnant at the time.

In black musical culture, performing at the famed Apollo was like returning to church. "For more than 75 years, entertainers, most of them African-American, have launched their careers, competed, honed their skills, and nurtured one another's talent at the Apollo Theater," wrote Lucinda Moore in Smithsonian magazine. They have generated breakthroughs in music and dance that have transcended race and, eventually, have changed popular entertainment."

The Apollo had previously been a whites-only burlesque club, but it opened to racially integrated audiences in 1934, with a wild reputation as a stage where performers sweat to gain the affection of a notoriously critical audience and a "executioner" shops undesirable acts away. Almost every important African American band of the era appeared during the first sixteen years of its existence, including many in the mid-1950s who helped mold the history of rock-and-roll music. When James Brown performed there in 1959, witnesses stated they could feel the entire structure pulsing.

But Tina's later presence would shake the building to its core. As Moore put it, "Wearing microscopic skirts and stiletto heels, she exuded a raw sex appeal on stage that far surpassed, and preceded, Madonna or Beyoncé, or anything they did to draw attention to risqué display." Later in the 1970s, the famed venue would close its doors due to heavy competition from larger arenas, such as Madison Square Garden (where Tina would also eventually play), and the theater Fortunately, in the 1980s, the Inner City Broadcasting Corporation purchased and refurbished it, securing its landmark status and reviving its famous amateur night events, which continue to thrive today.

According to Portia Maultsby, editor of the book African American Music, "it was a testing ground for artists, a second home, an institution within their community almost at the level of the black churches." Indeed, Tina returned the Apollo to testifying in a big way, and the Revue had passed into a kind of pop scripture by then.

Tina would do two classic things at the Apollo, in addition to singing the big songs of the day for her and Ike: she would testify and signify, almost gospel-funk-style, on behalf of James Brown, a hero of hers who had made that stage hallowed ground, while also staking out her own claim to a special place on that ground. In terms of emotion and pleading, she delivered a blazing performance of his "Please, Please Please" that virtually surpassed the original.

Their crossover timing couldn't have been better—or perhaps "luckier" is a better word. The big time was either approaching or had already arrived, almost too quickly to notice. So it had to be time for a little road trip to, where else, Las Vegas. Surprisingly, another coincidence occurred during this time period, one that would influence Tina's persona from then on, through her more hard rock and even later solo phases. This was her decision to bleach her hair while Ike was out of town, having returned to St. Louis to stand trial for an alleged bank robbery. Bleaching was a hot trend at the time, but Tina's hairdresser left the heat on for too long, and when the cap came off, virtually all of her reddish, kinky hair fell out.

Because of the hair incident, she had to wear a variety of blond-ish wigs to cover it up, which she quickly began to enjoy as a fashion statement, even encouraging the Ikettes to do the same so that all of their long locks would be twirling and swirling in unison during performances, another signature look she inadvertently created. Her sense of dress was as naturally theatrical as her singing.

Her music, with her characteristic howl, had also become associated with the Turner company. She now had "the look" to go with "the sound," and the show business roller coaster was picking up speed in ways she had never imagined. One of the great things about living in the digital age is that all of these original recordings, often with sparkling visuals to accompany them, are easily accessible on YouTube, and it's a stunning guided tour of her and their musical evolution to view and listen to these early songs in rapid succession.

Start with Ike's "Rocket 88" from 1951, then move on to "A Fool in Love," "Poor Fool," "I Idolize You," and "It's Gonna Work Out Fine" (with its witty spoken-word banter intoned not by Ike but by Mickey

Baker), all from 1961, and finally "I'm Blue" from 1962. The head-spinning acceleration of hits was delirious, as was the couple's relationship, which featured an ever-escalating torrent of those other kinds of hits for which Ike is now justly famous.

Tina clearly had a cognitive dissonance or disconnect at this point, making it appear impossible to distinguish one type of hit from another. Ike continued to apply his most effective approach for managing the women in his life who proved most valuable to his purposes and intentions, ignoring divorce (which was still more than a decade away). Following the birth of their son in 1960, he legally married her in 1962 to secure the name change he'd previously imposed on her.

Her mother in St. Louis was naively happy with the news, unaware of what was truly going on behind the scenes, aside from all the trappings of apparent success for her daughter. Meanwhile, Ike always maintained that he married Tina solely to keep her ex-boyfriend, fellow King of Rhythm Raymond Hill, from returning to her. But again, Ike made a lot of claims. Tina's marriage may not have been legal at all because it happened so quickly in Tijuana while he appeared to be married to another wife or two (or three).

Tina appeared to be in a constant state of shock, the kind that most people experience during actual battle and that leaves some victims with what we now term posttraumatic stress syndrome for years afterward. But it was thoroughly hidden and sublimated, driven well below the surface of her public life by that very tremendous surge of triumph. All she could do, she reasoned, was surf that wave.

Chance, as it always does, favored the well-prepared. Ike had been planning for this moment not just since he hit his stride ten years before with Jackie Brenston and his "Rocket 88," but also since he was a young deejay at WROX in Clarksdale and was educated at the piano bench by the great Pinetop Perkins. Ike always took from the greatest; for his first success, he borrowed from Pete Johnson and Big Bill Turner, and now he borrowed from Tina Turner. He was virtually tasting the big time with Tina providing the vocal chops he'd been missing with Bonnie and Annie earlier on, and his Ikettes providing the hot visual appeal and constant gymnastic gyrating. He wasn't going to let it go this time.

Timing was important, and it's something we can't even control, no matter how talented we are. The frenetic national dance crazes of 1962 and 1963 were likewise served up to Ike on a silver platter, with a youth-fueled demand for wild abstract dances with little physical contact between the two partners. Moves like the Twist, Pony, Stomp, Mashed Potato, Hully Gully, and Monkey were ideal for Tina's quivering legs now that she was being shadowed by her bewigged and mini skirt Ikettes.

The composer's limitations became clear when he began reusing earlier Ike rhythm-and-blues songs for the new pop period by simply dressing it up in bright new garments. It rarely went well for him. "Tra La La La La La" was a retread of Ike's previous theme tune "Prancing"; "You Shoulda Treated Me Right" hopped around wonderfully; "Sleepless" was a long, heavy-duty blues grind; and "I'm Blue" was released as the Ikettes' debut single, reaching number 19 in the pop charts in February 1962.

However, they all benefited enormously from the public's urge to dance dance dance. And while the crowds saw Tina and her girls spin in hot shimmy heaven, they imagined themselves to be dancing as well. She was a fictitious vital force for every tense libido. But suddenly her existence revolved around "The Tour," a never-ending merry-go-round that makes today's youthful "stars" look like a slow-motion cakewalk.

Of course, the only tours that were even remotely more frantic were those conducted by a certain new pop group called the Beatles in 1963-1964, a transcendentally talented pack of archetypal gods who brilliantly re-processed the jittery black rhythm-and-blues music of Chuck Berry and Little Richard for unsuspecting but hungry white audiences. The Ike and Tina Turner Revue, on the other hand, was able to approach the white audience with undiluted strength and grit. In the middle of Beatlemania, their tight little rocker "I Can't Believe What You Say" hit the top of the charts in 1964. "Top-most of the poppermost," as John Lennon famously remarked cynically.

The song is only one minute and forty-four seconds long, but Tina's shaking makes it feel like a week. An old concert film shows her shimmying in front of the band, with Ike jerking spasmodically behind her in his white gangster suit. It also showed us all without a doubt that she would soon be breaking out of his stylish kitchen and preparing her own cake. Of course, these were still peppy rhythm-and-blues pop tracks, and she was still four years away from her transition to serious rock music, which would come with songwriting assistance from Phil Spector in 1965 and John Fogerty in 1969.

When Ike's contract with Juggy Murray expired, he had the opportunity to move gears professionally, but rather than accept that it was Sue Records in general, and Murray in particular, that got him where he was, he began messing around again with the Bihari Brothers. He was always fond of double dealing, both with his women and with his business friends, so he signed a $40,000 advance with Juggy, bought a new property, but didn't supply anything that Murray could actually release. It was his traditional rope-a-dope maneuver.

Ike's beautiful ranch house in Valley Park Hills, on the outskirts of Los Angeles, was a haven for black musicians who made it big, like Ray Charles and Nancy Wilson. So when Ike earned some fresh income, he naturally decided to take a post in that elite enclave, and he brought his new and popular wife along with him to show her off as well. She brought her children, Craig and Ronald, from St. Louis, along with a woman to care for them while she returned to the circuit grind, back out on the unending road.

The Revue's approach to touring at this point was practically ritualistic: around ninety days and nights of clubs around Los Angeles, including the Cinnamon Cinder and the 5-4 Ballroom, and with black and white audiences in San Diego and San Francisco. This was followed by another ninety days and nights of mind-bending one-night-stand appearances across America, and following on the heels of that out-of-town binge came another ninety-day frenzy of local dates.

After a year of nonstop activity, the Revue would be given a special treat: one week off, but it would be a week during which Ike would make them all come in early for rehearsals and recordings. There were no roadies to assist, and the band members had to lug their own equipment everywhere. Nobody asked any questions, and nobody knew anything different or better. It was a mobile feast featuring a mobile beast.

It's always difficult dealing with the dark side of artists whose work is still so essential, as Aaron Cohen admitted to me. "While I would not excuse his heinous personal behavior, and I'm sure the stories about him are true, he was an incredible musician, a sharp songwriter, and he had a fantastic tremolo-laden guitar sound."He also continued to generate new musical ideas from the mid-1950s until the early 1970s, a feat shared by few. Ike was also a fantastic bandleader, and keeping these bands together while dealing with all of the roadblocks was no simple task (until his drug consumption got out of hand). It still amazes me that he could play 'Steel Guitar Rag' at the Chicago Blues Festival eighteen years ago. Meanwhile, whether working at Sun Records or seeing Annie Mae Bullock's promise, he was an influential scout for musical talent. But I'm not sure how to appropriately balance, acknowledge, and handle all of the good he accomplished for music with the devastation he caused to those around him." Who does it? It's a never-ending conundrum.

"Once again, James Porter wanted me to understand the full scope of Ike's brilliance as a player, which is often overlooked in the chaos of his personal life.Around 1969, Ike and Tina were completely realized as a "rock act." Back then, paying full respect to the blues was arguably the coolest thing you could do. Tina held herself as though she wanted you to know where the rock stars got it, and the songs were peppered with social commentary, sexual frankness, and references to getting high. This gave them a sense of identity for the rest of the 1970s (until their dissolution in 1976)."They'd found a stable home with Liberty/United Artists and developed a style that owed as much to earthy blues and rock experimentalism as it did to their earlier soul foundation. According to his own admission, Ike regarded himself more of a backstage guy, but during 'I Smell Trouble,' for once Ike is in the spotlight doing a lengthy guitar run, proving that he wasn't simply the equal of a Jimmy Page or a Jeff Beck, he was the source!"

The Ikettes, in particular, were usually pushed harder than everyone else and paid much less, which was ironic given that they were instrumental in Tina establishing the flashy and sexy fem aura for Ike. They morphed throughout the years into interchangeable goddess sculptures whose purpose it was to grab attention and be as ornamental as possible, in addition to being super athletic dancers of course. The original Ikettes were Robbie Montgomery, Venetta Fields, and Jessie Smith, who were ripped off from Lassiter's Artists and subsequently evolved into the Mirettes on their own.

Chafing at the continual strain and also under Ike's spell as his concubines, they broke out independently for a while in 1964-1966 with a run of respectable Modern Records hits: "The Camel Walk" in 1964 and "Peaches and Cream" and "I'm So Thankful" in 1965. They could be hefty, and some listeners have compared their swagger to the funk style exemplified later on by the gritty visionary Betty Mabry-Davis.

When "Peaches and Cream" became popular, Ike chafed and sent out a different group of Ikettes—Janice Singleton, Diane Rutherford, and Marquentta Tinsley—for a Dick Clark caravan of stars, while keeping Montgomery, Fields, and Smith for himself in the Revue. Tina would get backup vocals from Singleton and Rutherford on Phil Spector's next breakthrough smash, "River Deep, Mountain High."
Meanwhile, Ike hired various women as Ikettes over the years, including Pat Arnold, Juanita Hixon, Gloria Scott, Maxine Smith, and, later, Pat Powdrill, Ann Thomas, Shelly Clark, Rose Smith, Edna Richardson, Stonye Figueroa, Ester Jones, Claudia Lennear, Linda Sims, and Paulette Parker. They all deserve credit for working with Ike at all, and especially for allowing Tina to be Tina despite the constant difficulties caused by his flagrant infidelities.

Once she was free of Ike and on her own, she definitely abandoned the concept of Ikettes, instead referring to her dancers as "flowers." Nobody knows how any of them survived the demanding work schedule and internal stresses of that body-and-mind-punishing

Revue, but one other recreational aspect of the music business has always been open and evident for all to witness.

The Ikettes were fond of smoking joints to help their energy levels, and Ike often gave Benzedrine to Tina (who didn't approve of any "poisons" at all) to help (or force) her get through the constant vocal demands of his perpetual recording sessions.

Ironically, Ike was still exclusively a coffee-and-cigarettes kind of person, maybe some alco-fuel to pretend to relax, but, as previously said, he despised narcotics and fined or beat up his staff if they were caught using. I suspect that a control freak of his stature did not like the lack of control that narcotics entailed, at least not until he matured and discovered cocaine, which he snow-shoveled by the pound.

But, for some reason, he let his Ikettes consume dope whenever they wanted, possibly because he thought they were "special," and he even started supplying them with loads of pot on the road to keep them happy—or as happy as they could be while working for Mephistopheles. But, as the popularity of their "Peaches and Cream" outing grew, and nearly everyone in the industry wanted to offer the original Ikettes club appearances and recording gigs, Ike created a veritable revolving door of alternate Ikettes to keep them all in line during job insecurity.

The major Ikettes cleverly negotiated their way out of his possessive clutches in September 1965, when their sprightly but fundamentally Supremes-cloned single "I'm So Thankful" was soaring in the pop charts. greater and greater and even bigger things were looming on Ike and Tina Turner's joint horizon by then, with something deep and high—and completely insane—rapidly building in the wings. Phil Spector takes the stage to the left.

CHAPTER 4:
THE PUBLIC ROMANCER

It's always been about the music. His, theirs, and hers: it was a mind-boggling and joyful collaborative gift to musical culture. The amount of albums and shows produced and presented by Ike and Tina Turner, both together and as a solo act, is staggering. During their sixteen-year recording career, Ike and Tina Turner created several masterpieces in a variety of genres, evolving their artistic style and creative sensibilities from basic rhythm and blues with a soul inflection to more complex rock and roll with a bluesy feel and finally to a heavy-duty funk-rock mode with crossover pop appeal.

The sensually charged torch song structure of Tina, which encouraged listeners to abandon their troubles by getting up and dancing them away, was one factor that connected these disparate threads. Their music elicited an involuntary thrill similar to the religious rapture that gave rise to gospel, soul, and funk in the first place.

The other common thread between records is the perplexing fact that, while Ike was clearly a psychopath, he was also a very talented psychopath, with a knack for clever and snappy large-band arrangements, hyper stylized instrumentation, and frequently compelling production values, all of which were under his creative control from the start. By today's sluggish standards, all of this single-minded drive and wholehearted devotion to uninterrupted action is almost unfathomable.

The key to their best recordings (or at least one of them) is how connected they are to their live performances, which often overlap dramatically. Indeed, as famous as they are for studio records, they are even more widely appreciated as one of the most sizzling live acts in the entertainment field. This is due to the fact that they have been performing live more than 300 days per year since their inception. And, while many of their early and middle-period albums would appeal to fans of hard-core rhythm-and-blues music, the best ones they recorded were unquestionably their live albums, and that's where a new generation of listeners can discover what the big deal was all about.

The Ike and Tina Turner Revue Live at the Club Imperial and Harlem Club in St. Louis, 1964; The Ike and Tina Turner Show, 1965; In Person with the Ikettes, 1969; Ike and Tina Turner Festival of Performances, 1970; Live at Carnegie Hall, 1970; and The World of Ike and Tina Turner, 1973 are probably the highlights. Several instances of their best live CDs as barometers of their massive stage productions are certainly worth a cursory look.

In 1963, they began to boost the ante while still recording with Sue Records, producing Dynamite! In fast succession (speed was always of the essence with Ike).Ike produced the songs It's Gonna Work Out Fine, It's Gonna Work Out Fine, and Don't Play Me Cheap. They were already a smashing success by 1964, and they were one of the few American entertainers (along with the Beach Boys) who had a chance in hell of competing with the British invasion of the Beatles and the Rolling Stones, or, at the very least, holding their own in the face of their powerful cultural onslaught.

IKE AND TINA TURNER REVUE LIVE IN ST. LOUIS AT THE CLUB IMPERIAL

Kent Records released it in November 1964. Kings of Rhythm, Ike Turner, Tina Turner, Stacey Johnson, Vernon Guy, Venetta Fields, Jimmy Thomas, Bobby John, and Robbie Robinson are among the performers. Ike Turner was in charge of the production. The time is 35:49.

Please Please Please (James Brown and Johnny Terry) 6:54 / Feel So Good (Junior Parker) 3:12 / The Love of My Man (Ed Townsend) 3:55 / Think (Lowman Pauling) 2:24 / Drown in My Own Tears (Henry Glover) 7:31 / I Love the Way You Love (Berry Gordy) 3:12 / Your Precious Love (Jerry Butler) 2:30

The then-newly minted Ike and Tina Turner show would launch an endless series of club circuit appearances coupled with a rapid-succession release of singles and albums designed by Ike to fully capitalize on the obvious gold mine he had prospected for and found in his latest girlfriend and soon-to-be wife on October 27, 1959, at the Club Imperial in St. Louis. Despite being worshiped in a manner akin to the little cardboard billboard from his "Rocket 88" era, this famous venue is currently in danger of being demolished. This live recording catches some of the enticing fury of their early club concerts in St. Louis.

The Turners recorded some early tracks for later successful albums there, including Ike and Tina Turner Revue Live, and they played there regularly on Tuesday nights to praise. It's a spectacular example of their sheer strength, first released only in America and then distributed globally on various labels, then re-released as "Please Please Please" in 1968, with the CD issue adding additional tracks from the album Festival of Live Performances. This album was proudly labeled as "some of the early pop rock n' soul recordings that made this band a household name."

"Several years ago the recording industry was hit like an atomic bomb blast by the exciting songs of Ike and Tina Turner, if you missed this spectacular unit in action you can still be a witness, so if you think your heart can take it, drop this on the turntable and enjoy the greatest moments in their musical entertainment magic," Soul Magazine's promotion editor Warren Lanier observed in his liner notes about Tina. ..Tina, the bronze bombshell, erupted all over the Club Imperial stage. When closing up the Revue's presentation, she absolutely tears you apart and leaves you breathless." This is a terrific listening entrée into their searing world of early momentum for a band that is clearly headed aloft.

The years 1964 and 1965 were also notable for their significant contributions to the tricky format of live concert albums, which were not always the most dependable mode for even the best musicians but by far the best way to get as close to their sizzling live performance energy as possible without actually being in the theaters they rattled so emphatically. The best examples were Kent Records' Live: Ike and Tina Turner Revue Live and Ike and Tina Turner Show Vol. 2 on Loma Records, as well as the studio release Get It on

Cenco and an early Greatest Hits package on Sue Records, their former home.

Destiny would enter the fray once more, this time dressed as a great producer who used the entire recording studio as a single musical instrument. Phil Spector, a great musical innovator from the early and mid-1960s, invented a special sonic quality that made his records as distinct as they were memorable: booming, reverberating echo and massively lush orchestration, with gigantic chiming avalanches of sorrow and joy in equal measure in his melancholy girl groups. Spector's distinctive and hallmark enormous analog sound and furious doubling up of instrumentation gave those sorrowful little two-minute pop symphonies both charm and long-lasting technical prowess to the Ronettes, Shirelles, Crystals, Shangri-Las, and others. The hugely popular Righteous Brothers hits were among Spector's other historic achievements in the same domain, all of which used what had by then become his own personal brand, often imitated but never duplicated: big, shimmering architectural monuments to the raw emotional impact of overwhelming, reverberating sound waves. He was one of the first and finest examples of the producer as an artist in popular music, and he was well known in the business for establishing his own distinct sonic atmosphere. And it would be Spector, already a historic creative titan at the time, who would help to completely renovate and re-launch the Ike and Tina Turner Revue, ushering in their unexpected rock era.

As usual, two unrelated elements came together like alchemy to accomplish this: first, the Turners had reached an impasse with their usual brand of boogie-blues rock and roll, particularly within the limited scope of Ike as a songwriter; and second, Spector had been around and at the top of his game for so long that song styles and tastes were shifting slightly away from his earlier boy-meets-girl/bad-boy-woos-girl sonic soap operas. Spector's contribution to the future of music was his gifted use of clearly white arrangements sung by voices that were in some cases blacker in tone than even Motown could muster, while regularly employing well-tempered jazz musicians as his pop posse, most notably the famous Wrecking Crew session geniuses Hal Blaine and Carol Kane. He then processed everything via a torrent of disorienting audio effects known as the "Spector wall of sound," which may paralyze the mind while liberating the heart.

Mark Ribowsky opened his excellent study of Spector and his historic influence, He's a Rebel: Rock and Roll's Legendary Producer, with this single salient fact: "Phil Spector, a little man with a Napoleon complex, faced his own private Waterloo in early 1966," referring to the fact that by that year, Spector had all but worn out his welcome on the world music stage and needed to craft a new and even more elaborate m His background had already earned him the title of musical deity, but soon enough, and entirely unexpectedly, Ike and Tina would move into the aural church that Phil had built— all for one incredible song.

"Phil Spector did overdub background vocals on his records to create a swirl of voices that aped his instrumental tracks, but his true love was live music, a rhythm section blaring and wailing its brains out," Ribowsky writes, "a rhythm section blaring and wailing its brains out."

"At Gold Star Sound Studios in Hollywood, a titanic rhythm section of the kind Spector was famous for—four guitars, three basses, three pianos, two drums, and a small army of percussion—became one, as only a live, massed monolith could." Gold Star's Studio A was soaked in sine waves, which bounced off the walls and the low ceiling before tumbling out of two echo chambers and being sucked onto a tape machine.

"When mixed down, the sound was not of this world, and it wasn't a melody in the traditional sense." It was a feeling, a mood, aural poetry, and pure rock-and-roll bliss. Even the ludicrous teenage themes of Spector's early records sound like the Ride of the Valkyries elevated to Valhalla by a tide of inspired commotion that was the Wall of Sound, or as Spector himself would have preferred, 'a Wagnerian approach to rock and roll, little symphonies for kids.'" This was a nearly ideal description of what would later become the Turners' breakaway shifting of gears in 1966, "River Deep, Mountain High."

Spector was born in the big-band era of 1940, and he was just twenty-five years old when he forever changed the face of popular music with a never-ending series of tunes that topped the charts twenty-seven times between 1961 and 1965. One of his later hits, the Righteous Brothers' huge, booming anthem of sorrow, "You've Lost That Lovin' Feeling," was perhaps most personally telling for Ike and Tina Turner. "Spector was a visionary, not a revolutionary," Ribowsky clarified, "He didn't change the system, he used it." What Spector did was not invent a new kind of rock and roll, but he brilliantly enhanced the old one, using the same simple song.

In Tom Wolfe's article "The First Tycoon of Teen" for the New York Herald Tribune in 1965, during a time when the Beatles' Rubber Soul was causing seismic musical shifts, Spector was already having to defend his deceptively simple songwriting approach to operating as the American Mozart. "This music has a spontaneity that is not found in any other type of music, and it is what is here now." It's unjust to lump it in with rock & roll and condemn it. You know what I mean? It's really current. Actually, it's more in the style of the blues. It's blues pop."

Pop blues became possibly the finest term to characterize what Ike and Tina Turner were already doing at the time. It was generally sped up into a furious dance tempo, yet it remained a female blues twist on the classic torch poetic genre. The bluesy torch ballad is a distinct genre, one that would be carefully treated again and again by great female vocalists throughout the 1960s and 1970s, right up to Tina's churning and flaming anthems of angst.

Tina's extraordinary vocal abilities were also tailored to the Spector sound, which can best be described as a gigantic vibrating wall: ambient, echoing, reverberating, shimmering, sweet, dark, brooding, menacing, and finally hyper melodramatic. Spector's reimagining of the classic torch song for Tina's voice and soul was a tidal wave of desires denied, postponed, or derailed—a perfectly crafted heartbreaker aria, the spiritually anguished sound of mini-operas about desperately trying to win back someone you've lost but can't let go.

But by the time Tina Turner got her hands on that torch, entrusted to her by eccentric recording pioneer Phil Spector, it sounded like nothing anyone in the world had ever heard before.

In 1965, Ike and Tina Turner had signed with their twelfth record label, often more than one at a time due to Ike's grasping tendencies. Loma Records was a modest Warner Bros. subsidiary run by Bob Krasnow, a genuinely sympathetic white admirer of black music who had briefly worked with the great James Brown. However, given the current political climate, Brown believed it was inappropriate for him to be working with a white producer, so Krasnow was on the hunt for a similarly dynamic black artist to get behind.

Tina Turner, as a female James Brown, who Krasnow noticed had the strength of Mr. Dynamite but far better looking legs, is the only performer I can envision him encountering who may match the bill. After touring every day of the year and doing about five high-octane performances a night, the band was so tight that he was more than willing to record a handful of songs for them, none of which charted. That's when the similarly restless Phil Spector called, looking for a new way to alter the music world for the third or fourth time.

When asked if he and his crew had Ike and Tina on board, Krasnow was astonished to hear Phil's high-pitched lips say that he wanted to create a record—with Tina. The emphasis is on the term "Tina." Krasnow, like everyone else in the know, held Spector in awe for all the proper reasons. As 1965 came to a conclusion, he had already had 10 major successes with the Righteous Brothers when the laid-back duo chose to leave him and sign with Verve Records. For similar reasons, artists could only work with Spector for so long until they burnt out or collapsed. He was the only music professional I could think of who could be as insane as Ike.

Nonetheless, he was and still is acclaimed for his almost mystical sound producing skills (despite serving a life sentence for murder), and at this juncture of his career, he needed a boost. A buddy had advised that he see Ike and Tina at the Galaxy Club on Sunset Boulevard, and he was taken aback, which was unusual for a pro of his caliber. He instantly added them to the list for his own revue at the Moulin Rouge, which had a slightly schizoid lineup of other performers, including the Byrds, the Lovin' Spoonful, Ray Charles, Petula Clark, and Donovan.

He went to the fabled Brill Building in New York to collaborate with the supersonic pop maestro duo of Jeff Barry and Ellie Greenwich (writers of such monsters as "Be My Baby," "Baby I Love You," "Chapel of Love," "Leader of the Pack," and "Do Wah Diddy") and returned with a hit song. Darlene Love, for whom he wrote "A Fine, Fine Boy," enjoyed what she heard of his new secret music, but he explained that it wasn't quite her thing. Tina was supposed to do this. He didn't say "Ike and Tina's thing." Instead, he worked out some business terms with Krasnow, reportedly offering Ike $25,000 (reminiscent of Juggy Murray's old offer of a stately sum to work with Tina as well) to let him have Tina and her voice and for Ike never to set foot in the studio during the process of making "River" into what he thought—or hoped—would be his pièce de résistance, his masterwork. Tina adored the song, especially because it wasn't the traditional simple-structured Ike rhythm-and-blues format, but rather a sophisticated tower of rock force, and especially because it wasn't written by Ike and he'd have no role in its creation.

That process was opaque, as it often was with Spector, with Phil amassing acres and acres of instruments before exploding headfirst into a scorching conclusion of unbelievable intensity. She couldn't conceive how her voice would be audible amid this complicated roar at first, but she hadn't yet experienced the unearthly ability with which he could manage vocals as expertly as musicians and their instruments. She estimated that there were 75 players in the studio at any given time until she finally made a rough vocal recording for him to utilize after so many takes and retakes that she lost count (nearly losing consciousness as well).

Krasnow, the head honcho of Loma Records who would later become the head honcho at Elektra Records, recalls being surprised by Ike's treatment of his obvious gold mine of a brilliant singer when they met at this time, as described in Vanity Fair. "He treated her like she was his maid, she was in the kitchen with a wet rag, down on her hands and knees wiping the floor wearing another rag on her head." Tina was Ike's maid in more ways than one.

Krasnow encountered a person who most people saw, someone with a sensual public demeanor but private mores that are rather old fashioned and archaic. Tina could be your girlfriend, your sister, your best friend—all of these emotional markers could be fulfilled at the same time if you met her. However, when she performs, she has the ability to dramatically arouse you by bringing songs to life in a way that is completely hers.

Phil Spector shared many similarities with Ike Turner, including a prodigy background and an intense bond with his own lead singer, Ronnie Spector (née Bennett). According to Krasnow, "at one point Phil had every single big studio musician in Hollywood in there, and of course, most of the famed Wrecking Crew, with Hal Blaine and the brilliant bassist Carol Kane."

All of this for a single track, a single side of a single, or even a full album. "River Deep, Mountain High" was a Spector masterpiece, with a sound so deep and heavy that you almost forgot you were listening to music. There's no other way to describe Ike's reaction when he finally heard the track. He was so taken aback that he couldn't put it into words; this was in another league entirely, if not another world. He was really disappointed, to use a musician's term. He believed it was impossible, perhaps because it is generally impossible.

Tina is widely acknowledged to have given the best performance of her life for this eccentric producer. Spector took months to complete the pressing he was satisfied with, as per his usual obsessive technical laboring, with Krasnow reporting that he was brought sixteen different pressings to consider, each more compelling than the last, which, as he put it at the time, only dogs could hear the differences on.

"River Deep, Mountain High" was eventually ready to be released in the late spring of 1966, during the golden musical moment in which the Beatles released Revolver. In fact, George Harrison thought it one of the most perfect recordings ever recorded, a pop song so brilliantly created that nothing could be done to improve on it.

Indeed, Spector, who was never known to be modest, was reasonably positive that this song would be Ike and Tina's first number one chart-topping hit and enthusiastically informed them so. Surprisingly, to many at the time (but practically everyone else since), it wasn't—it was a complete flop, at least by Spector standards. Larry Levine, the renowned audio engineer who had collaborated with him on the overall design of his wall of sound, was also taken aback by the lackluster response of most music trade newspapers.

He felt that Spector, the boy wonder who had gathered perhaps twenty-five chart-topping records in a succession, was ready for some sizing down by reviewers and industry types. Other producers, artists, and the general music-loving public, of course, saw and heard things very differently. It was accepted as the gleaming manufacturing and performance pinnacle that it truly is. Nonetheless, it did not sell well. During the summer, it peaked at number 88 on the pop charts before beginning to fall.

Spector was devastated and heartbroken. Phil, according to Levine, withdrew into himself, didn't want to compose any more music, and just kind of permanently fled behind his now famous black glasses and hid away in self-imposed mute exile.

As recounted in "New Musical Express", when Spector first played the intended Tina song for her, singing along on a guitar, she was mesmerized: "Wow! Jack Nitzsche's arrangement was truly unique! The Jeff Barry/Ellie Greenwich/Phil tune knocked me out." Tina was still astounded after all of her efforts on the song "River Deep," particularly by the incredible complexity of its recording style.

"He was so much behind that project—it was something he strongly, strongly believed in," she said in the Best of Tina DVD video about its sonic architecture. I have to tell you, it was an army of supporting vocals—a choir. The place was packed with vocalists." But, despite (or perhaps because of) its complexity, the industry couldn't relate to it, and audiences were perplexed by its waves of instruments and voices. Tina Turner's historical statements on the official Tina Turner website explained why: "It was too black for the pop stations and too pop for the black stations." But it did show folks what I was capable of."

"We were breaking the chains that were holding us back from a mass audience," she said, referring to a white audience, with her version of the song's B-side, "A Love Like Yours," which became a number 16 hit in the United Kingdom. All she had to do now was find a way to free herself from the bonds that bound her to her thuggish pimp. Of course, it was a difficult journey, especially given her own sense of loyalty, whatever wrong it may have been.

She felt obligated to be faithful to Ike during the first seven years of her troubled existence with him because of how he had assisted her in the beginning. Naturally, she found it impossible to separate his attitude and behavior from what he had done for her professionally, but her perplexity was exacerbated by fear, much as everyone else in his clique shared his curiously compelling grasp on people.

This strange cult-like environment was noticed publicly by a large number of individuals in their circle: the fact that he commanded his roost through a brutal intimidation so extreme that if any of his own band breached some of his compulsive rules, they may be fined, fired, assaulted, or pistol-whipped.

Tina was naturally dissatisfied by the song's public and critical reception, believing that it was the beginning of a whole new side of her musical identity (which it was, as time would demonstrate), but that the audience wasn't quite ready for such a bold evolutionary leap.

As is typically the case with musical releases in one country or another, "River Deep" was a big hit in Europe, where there was always a bigger desire for black music in general, inventive pop in particular, and notably a dish called Tina. Regardless of how it was received in some places, 1966 was their most creative and commercial turning point, especially for Tina, who had personally dived so deep and reached so high.

DEEP RIVER, HIGH MOUNTAIN

It was released in 1966. Records from London. Gold Star Studios was used for recording. Phil Spector and Ike Turner produced the album. Tina Turner on vocals, Barney Kessel on guitar, Carol Kaye on bass, Jim Gordon on drums, Claudia Lennear and Bonnie Bramlett on backing vocals, and Harold Battiste on piano. Larry Levine is an engineer. Jack Nitzsche, Barry Page, and Perry Botkin arranged the music. Dennis Hopper appears on the cover. Time taken: 37:06.

(Jeff Barry, Phil Spector, Ellie Greenwich) River Deep, Mountain High I Idolize You (Ike Turner) 3:38 3:46 / Eddie Holland & Lamont Dozier - A Love Like Yours 3:05 / Ike Turner's "A Fool in Love" Make Em Wait (Ike Turner) 3:33 Hold On Baby (Jeff Barry, Ellie Greenwich, and Phil Spector) 2:22 Save the Last Dance for Me (Doc Pomus, Mort Shuman) 2:59 Oh Baby (Ike Turner) 3:02 Every Day I Have to Cry (Arthur Alexander) 2:46 2:40 / Ike Turner's "Such a Fool for You" 2:48 / Everything's Gonna Be Fine (J. Michael Lee, Joe Seneca) You're So Fine (Lance Finney, Bob West, Willie Schofield) (3:14) 3:14

River Deep, Mountain High is a stunning studio recording peak that clocks in at 37 minutes and six seconds of pure aural splendor, with Spector meticulously handcrafting the title tune at Gold Star Studios. It was reissued in 1969 on A&M Records with a changed track listing and song choices, with Ike sharing producer duties for the first time in both their careers. Pitchfork ranked it 40th out of the top 200 records released in the 1960s. It's a good spot for the inexperienced to start exploring their mutual collaboration.

I've always admired Ben Fong-Torres' observations of Tina in general, and this record in particular, as he explored it in Rolling Stone back in 1971, when the song's impact was still raw. "To hear that song for the first time, in 1967, in the first year of acid-rock and Memphis soul, to hear that wall of sound falling toward you, with

Tina teasing it along, was to understand all the power of rock and roll." It was released in England in 1966 and reached number two, however it did not chart in the United States. 'It was exactly like my farewell,' claims Phil Spector. 'I was just saying goodbye, and I just wanted to go crazy for a few minutes—four minutes on wax,' she says. Unfortunately, that's always felt like Phil's attempt to explain away why his homeland didn't exactly understand what he was up to. Ben's appreciation for Tina's genuine superstar status is also quite adept, placing her in the pop and rock pantheon where she belongs, near the Rolling Stones, owing to the fact that many people compare Tina Turner to Mick Jagger when she's onstage. Tina, on the other hand, is far more aggressive and animalistic than even Mick when studied carefully. She commands whatever stage she is on.

Tina's response in Phil Agee's book Tina Pie that no matter what happened to her personally, "I always go on," was equally illuminating given what the couple was going through at the time. When I walk on stage, I drop whatever is troubling me, no matter how horrible it is. You know that type of hypnosis—I'm not sure what it's called—in which you put yourself into a trance? Self-hypnosis? That's all there is to it. I forget because I mesmerize myself."

However, the unique aural sensibilities of "River Deep" had to contend with themselves that same year, via the familiar-sounding Soul of Ike and Tina Turner, published on Kent again, which by then was far from anything instantly recognizable as soul music. With Festival of Live Performances on Kent in 1967, they proved to be masters of live concert CDs once more, and 1968 brought Ike and Tina Turner to London and the quiet little rocker So Fine to Pompeii. But 1969 would be their unforgettable year.

British musicians who were extremely captivated with black blues and rhythm-and-blues sounds by singers such as BB King and Tina Turner were set to go on a fall tour of the United Kingdom, no less brilliant than the Rolling Stones. Mick, Keith, and the boys felt it would be a great idea to bring the entire Ike and Tina Turner Revue to open for them in their large-scale shows. Tina Turner began to firmly consolidate her newfound reputation as a Rock Goddess with them.

That, combined with a live U.S. clip of Tina performing "River Deep" on the English Top of the Pops television program, launched Tina on her path to rock royalty, with Ike now more or less along for the ride, a disgruntled figure in the shadows as the spotlight shone brightly on her. Despite Ike's protracted descent into obscurity, which he had mainly inflicted on himself, the up-and-coming Rolling Stones were already ready, willing, and able to give Tina the respect she deserved.

Porter also stressed to me the impassioned motivation that later so-called rock bands, particularly white ones like the Stones, would draw from their apparently milder forefathers. "Historically, when white rockers drew inspiration from R&B, it was usually with an emphasis on the raw and raunchy." Otis Redding, for example, might be better suited to a garage-rock approach than Jerry Butler. With their high-energy live shows and guitar-based sound, Ike & Tina were a natural for rock bands to pick up on. Despite the formal precision of a Las Vegas spectacle, Ike's guitar and Tina's screaming voice exploded with rock & roll dynamite. They were an obvious choice to open for the Rolling Stones and eventually to headline rock festivals and ballrooms."

Apart from Mick Jagger confessing that she taught him how to dance properly onstage, Keith Richards had a not-so-secret crush on Tina when they met on tour. Onstage, he is frequently seen virtually ogling her bravery. It was almost as if she dragged the British rock band so in love with black blues music back to theater school and taught what show business was truly all about.

Richards was also clear about what made the Turner Revue so unique. He realized it was all Tina's fault, not the phony Svengali Ike fancied himself to be. Ike clearly envisioned himself as the next Phil Spector, the driving force behind the star. He was also a power of a different sort, a violent pimp capable of pistol-whipping musicians in his own band—someone you don't want to be around, let alone mess with.

Richards' Stone, bassist Bill Wyman, was especially fond of dating young Ikettes, and he agreed on Image Entertainment's Best of DVD, "I heard horrendous stories from The Ikettes about what was going on in the background." It was nearly unbelievable, in fact. The Ikettes changed so quickly that every time you saw them, it was an entirely different set because they couldn't deal with what was going on."

Despite its stylistic grandeur, there is a fundamental irony in this Spector signature song being written for her, if not about her, because it's odd sentiment is quite telling: "When you were a young boy, did you have a puppy that always followed you around, well I'm gonna be as faithful as that puppy, no I'll never let you down."

Following her instantly legendary working relationship with Spector and the incredible song that he birthed, all future producers they worked with had to step up their technical game. This was not a conscious decision or effort on their side; it was simply a change in the soundscape that became a natural new addition to their sonic landscape. Each song after this one, of course, tended to be larger in scope and scale, with a good example being their upcoming version of the wonderful John Fogerty song "Proud Mary," a song that is now much more associated with her than his own Creedence Clearwater Revival version. Needless to say, all of Tina's solo records once she broke free from Ike had to be produced in the most lavish manner possible.

Although Spector was devastated by the lukewarm response to his volcanic masterpiece, Tina took it in stride, content simply to be able to break out on her own (as co-producer) and away from her increasingly paranoid spouse. Meanwhile, Ike was probably content with only having the Phil incident, during which he had little power over the project or his wife. In his claustrophobic mentality, no matter how bright everyone said this intruder was, there was only room for one rooster in the yard.

The near-mystical connotations with Spector persisted, but in the music industry, with his mythology only flowering once, he withdrew to his castle overlooking Sunset Boulevard. When Rolling Stone editor Jan Wenner asked him how he managed to so skillfully create the sonic environments in which only his records thrived, his answer was typically both laconic and bombastic: "When I went into the studio, I created the sounds that I wanted to hear." His unique Tina sound was still a big hit in England, where the Rolling Stones took them on tour for twelve straight dates in September-October, in addition to another twelve or so on the road.

The Stones' tour began with a live concert at Albert Hall, which was simultaneously being recorded for Got Live If You Want It. The crowd erupted into a near-riot after six songs, with enthusiastic fans swarming the stage, a stunning sight of a whole new world for Ike and Tina, who were fundamentally down-home chitlin'-circuit veterans at heart, suddenly catapulted into pop at the top. Tina got along well with the bad boys of rock and roll, especially Mick Jagger, who believed in having an opening act that challenged his own band to up their game in order to beat them, which Tina readily achieved.

Apart from embracing their devotion as an early black rock and roller who had inspired them in the first place, Ike didn't get along with Jagger or Richards, as was customary. He could get into adoration; comparable respect, on the other hand, was something else entirely. He was also irritated by the fact that Jagger, Richards, and Wyman were all dating his Ikettes, as that form of rooster competition irritated him much more than the musical variety.

Tina saw England as a chance to finally see a future existence beyond Ike, what she regarded as a new life, a new way of living, of being. And the more she appeared on non-Ike-controlled indie venues and performances, such as the popular Ready Steady Go!The more she saw, the more she enjoyed what she saw, especially because the enormous new white audiences were focused mostly on her and her fellow singers and dancers and less on her dark glowering puppet master.

One of the psychics she constantly sought advice from for direction in her life and work even predicted that she would become a megastar and that her spouse would fall away like a leaf from a tree. The psychic allegedly saw the number 6, which apparently informed Tina that even though Ike was beating her up more frequently, she should hang on for another six days, six weeks, or six months, which transformed into another six years.

So she held on, through the Stones' follow-up tour, into France and Germany, and a slew of press and television interviews. Fans and critics alike admired her lively stage presence while also admiring her gentle, humble approach to the entire carnival she was living in. The frantic traveling continued—that was naturally where the major money was in the business anyway, which kept Ike off her back while he counted his money. The road was still the same old show industry grind, with one new twist: the press was now continuously following her, admiring her style, personality, and music. Following "River Deep," she was viewed not only as an important element of the Turner Revue, but also as the central sun around which they all revolved.

Ike's label hopping continued into 1969, with Cussing', Cryin', and Carryin' On on Pompeii, Get It Together and Get It-Get It on Cenco, His Woman, Her Man on Capitol, and In Person on Minit, the only album to achieve good sales, reaching number 142 on Billboard—a cyclone of compositions. Of course, the bigger she became, the angrier Ike became, resorting to twisted wire coat hangers as his weapon of choice in his rage attacks on her.

Privately, Tina's sadness had deepened into a troubling gloom as early as 1968, the ominous year preceding her Stones victory. That year, on what she described as "an ordinary day," she reached her breaking point and attempted suicide in private. Ike had gotten her pregnant yet again, but so had one of his non singing Ikettes, Ann Thomas, who had been one of her friends, supporters, and protectors before entering the Ike cult. Tina made the decision right then and there that she would not give birth to another of his children and instead chose to abort the pregnancy.

Around this period, he began to exhibit truly crazy and frightening actions, compounded by his increasingly extensive drug use, resorting once to clobbering her with his guitar, breaking it, then complaining that she had ruined his guitar and using his fists again. She told those who would listen that Ike had lost his wits by this point, beating her with phones, shoes, and his favored coat hangers.

He punched her in the face and shattered her jaw right before a show once, but she had to go onstage and sing anyway, straining to pronounce the words gurgled in the blood streaming around in her mouth. She was prepared to die, she was certain. She went to her family doctor, complaining of a nonexistent sleep issue, and asked for fifty exceedingly strong medications. She got a glass of water in the bathroom on her way to a club with her entire entourage and swallowed all fifty of them at once.

The medications kicked in while she was in the backseat of the limo, and the entire crew rushed her to Daniel Freeman Hospital in Inglewood, California, where she immediately needed her stomach pumped. When she eventually awoke, his face was staring at her. She wasn't sure if she was dead or alive until he yelled that she was attempting to ruin his life. Fifty years later, in My Love Story, she clearly recalled the strange experience of being resurrected against her will.

She explained how the emergency medical personnel acted. Ike supposedly requested if he could talk to her while pounding her tummy but was unable to get her to respond. Her subconscious mind heard him (she said), the voice broke through the fog, and her heart started racing again. The doctors told him to keep talking and that they had a pulse, and the next thing she remembered, she was in a hospital bed, wondering why she was there. She fell asleep again and awoke the next day, staring at Ike Turner and telling her, "You should die, you motherfucker."

"As soon as I got out of the hospital, he made me go back to work." I was exhausted, had awful stomach cramps, and had to smile my way through the entire event. When we were completed, the Ikettes led me to the changing room. Ike was angry again, 'You should die motherfucker,' he snarled. 'But you know what you'd do to me if you died.'"

That's when she went from disliking the man to fearing the man to hating the man, the man who had practically pulled her out of high school and launched her into an admittedly fascinating (at first) merry-go-round of music and show business. "When I awoke, I was dissatisfied. But I never attempted again because I had a revelation that changed the path of my life. I emerged from the darkness convinced that I was intended to live. I'd come for a cause. "I knew there was only one way out of this nightmare: through the door."

Tina Turner was like a thoroughbred racehorse who couldn't or wouldn't stop running. It was surely not lost on her that Sydney Pollack's They Shoot Horses Don't They? was one of the most adventurous and popular pictures released in 1969. But, for her, 1969 was the same mix of fantastic and horrible, great and dreadful, because they were finally getting the big jobs in Las Vegas, in the same International Hotel lounge where Elvis Presley was staging his own massive comeback.

As again, it was producer Bob Krasnow who emerged out of nowhere like some musical angel and provided her a song he thought she could do wonders with: Otis Redding's "I've Been Loving You Too Long" (which Ike despised and didn't want her to do, possibly for obvious reasons). Krasnow and his instincts were as accurate as they had always been. Tina delivered that Redding song with almost unbearable longing and anguish, and it became one of their biggest hits in years, reaching number 68 on the mainstream charts in May 1969.
It was also included on an accompanying album, Outta Season, along with other scorching blues tracks. Once again, she provided a cover rendition of a song that she completely stole from the original and made her own. Krasnow then created further momentum for the couple, particularly for her, by having The Hunter follow that hit in quick succession, giving more chart hits, including the title song as well as one that became a type of symbolic signature song for her: "Bold Soul Sister."

While the Woodstock event captured the attention of the nation and the world in the summer of 1969, the Turners were on a veritable binge of often overlapping releases, sent out into the airwaves as if the world was about to end. They weren't on the Woodstock list, but they did play a comparable hippie celebration in October, the Lake Amador Gold Rush celebration, with a slightly more blues and folk flavor and a healthy and respectable but not as out-of-control audience of roughly 50,000 spectators.

They were going places, as they always did, but for Tina, it was places she'd already gone with Ike, tried-and-true but stale rhythm-and-blues compositions with catchy but limited appeal to her rapidly expanding tastes. As if on cue, her old British pals the Rolling Stones appear. They had surpassed, if not surpassed, their contemporaries the Beatles, who were attempting to create their final masterpiece before splitting up into independent careers at the time.

In August 1969, the Stones released "Honky Tonk Woman," and the Beatles released "Come Together," their iconic Abbey Road opener, around the same time. Tina was keen to perform both songs onstage, which completely perplexed Ike, who was now stylistically far behind her. 1969 was also a banner year for rock and pop music in general, not just for the significantly new incarnation of Ike and Tina Turner's Revue taking shape, but for rock and pop music in general throughout the charts.

This was also the beginning of Tina's preferences seriously changing and maturing, pushing well beyond her relatively conservative husband's understanding of what music was, what it could be, and where it was headed. She began listening to rock music, thanks to the Stones and others, who were reinterpreting and repackaging musical ideas that were originally black. "Honky Tonk Women," a song that must have felt like it was written for and about her, a boisterous southern babe singing in seedy juke joints, was a game changer for her career in terms of style.

When the Stones asked her (and the Revue, of course) to join them on their U.S. tour to promote Let It Bleed and introduce their new guitarist, Mick Taylor, late of many a great British blues bands, such as John Mayall's, to replace their recently deceased founder, Brian

Jones, it was the perfect opportunity to try out what she considered her new black rock vibe in front of the ideal music lovers for her new spirit.

The tour would visit thirteen cities and perform eighteen gigs, beginning in November at the Los Angeles Forum, and would be documented for a theatrical documentary. Along with the reigning British rulers of modern pop music, one of their old black idols, BB King, and one of their new black heartthrobs, Tina Turner and her girls and her band, would be on the program. Ralph Gleason, one of our most significant pop reviewers of the time, summarized the whole thing best, I believe, in the new small music magazine he had just co-founded: Rolling Stone.

The second night's performance, at the Oakland Coliseum, he described as an intense experience that "may very well have been the best rock show ever presented." Gleason praised BB King, who was followed by Ike and Tina Turner's Revue, who came before Mick and the boys. Gleason was without a doubt the most stunning female performer on any contemporary stage at the moment.

One can only imagine her husband's reaction to such accolades, and especially Gleason's reaction to Tina's other showstopper: the Otis Redding song that Ike despised the most. "The climax of her act was the most blatantly sexual number I have ever seen at a concert," she famously said, while twisting and squirming and letting forth animalistic vocal screams that closely imitated orgasm.
It would be a performance that would later be included in the Stones' film Gimme Shelter, and one that she would find difficult to live down for many years afterward, thinking not only that she had gone too far, but also that Ike was behind her in the shadows, trying to capture some of her attention with his own grunting and groaning sounds. She thought the whole thing was awkward and nearly sexual, but the audience loved it.

Fortunately for Tina and her band (yes, it was now genuinely hers), they missed the infamous later Stones show at Altamont Speedway near San Francisco, where four people were killed, but the Stones tour nevertheless added rocket fuel to their upward momentum.

When 1970 rolled around, Ike and Tina were still buzzing from their exposure to an enormous white rock audience, with "Bold Soul Sister" hitting number 59 on the pop charts in January of the new year, a year packed with an ever-increasing public visibility for both the Revue and Tina in particular.

Ike signed a new deal with Minit Records, a subsidary of United Artists, which would represent them for the rest of their tenure together. Meanwhile, Tina's two favorite songs, "Honky Tonk Women" and "Come Together," were combined into a single that peaked at number 57 on the pop charts. Tina had been correct once more. Both of those songs were on an album that lingered on the charts for nineteen weeks, a fantastic run. Ike was kept busy counting his money, which he kept close to him in crammed luggage.

Ike was so preoccupied with counting that he didn't see his wife's health was rapidly deteriorating. Her doctor advised her to reduce her workload, but "Doctor" Ike advised her to continue despite suffering bronchitis (never fun for a singer), which turned out to be tuberculosis, prompting rounds of biopsies and spinal taps that revealed glandular infections and a collapsed lung. When she awoke in the hospital, there were flowers from "Mick Jagger and the Rolling Stones" but no flowers from her spouse.

Her disease remained for very some time, and it looks that it never truly left her. How could it, given that she was immediately back on the road, stuffed with antibiotics, performing at many planned events with a few extra gigs crammed in between those ones by Ike? They made regular appearances in Las Vegas to open for Elvis, which was obviously a tremendous deal for any musician, anywhere, at any time, especially Ike, who fancied himself as an artist with the same degree of power as the King.

The only problem was that all the attention was going to his Queen Tina. And Ike was becoming increasingly agitated as he made more money and had more drugs to spend it on. In his delirious mind, it was definitely time to build his own recording studio so he could publicly demonstrate that he, too, could be a Spector (more like a specter, in his case).

Yet on top of everything, they still had time to record and release a machine-gun-like series of albums: Cussin', Cryin' and Carryin' On on Pompeii, Get It-Get It on Cenco, Her Man, His Woman on their new home (or one of them at least) of Capitol, Outta Season on Blue Thumb, Ike and Tina Turner and the Ikettes—In Person on Minit, The Fantastic Ike and Tina on Sunset, Get It Together on Pompeii, and, rounding out the year, The Hunter on Blue Thumb again.

In 1970 and 1971, they released their competing "together" singles, Come and Workin' on Liberty, as well as three incredible live performance records: Live: On Stage in Paris on Liberty, Live at Carnegie Hall: What You Hear Is What You Get on United Artists, and Live: Something's Gotta Hold on Me on Harmony. But it would be the live recorded brilliance of their Carnegie Hall performance that audiences today would benefit the most from seeing. That one captures the spirit of her lightning in a bottle all by itself.

TINA AND IKE WHAT YOU HEAR LIVE AT CARNEGIE HALL IS WHAT YOU GET.

United Artists released it in July 1971. Ike and Tina Turner are the Kings of Rhythm. Ike Turner and Bonnie Barrett produced the film. The video lasts 59:26 minutes.

Bert Berns and Jerry Ragovoy's "Piece of My Heart" Everyday People (Sly Stone) 3:38 2:10 / Tina Turner Style Sweet Soul Music (Arthur Conley) 1:20 1:00 / Wilson Pickett's Ooh Poo Pah Doo Honky Tonk Women (Mick Jagger and Keith Richards) 4:05 3:05 / Ed Holland's A Love Like Yours Proud Mary (John Fogerty) 3:43 I Smell Trouble (Jessie Hill) 9:50 7:57 / Jeff Beck's I Want to Take You Higher I've Been Loving You For Too Long (Otis Redding, Jerry Butler) 3:35 Respect (Otis Redding) 8:35 5:03

Making it in your hometown is one thing, but New York, New York, has always been and always will be the place to be. If you can make it there, you can make it anywhere, as the popular song memorably proclaimed. However, their triumphal reappearance on August 15, 1971, was a great gem in terms of documenting that New York rise live on vinyl. The live recording they produced of their concert at Carnegie Hall is a live masterpiece, as well as a crash course in what made them outstanding as a performing ensemble.

After commanding the revered African American venue of the Apollo, the only conceivable place to top it would be the equally revered Carnegie Hall, where she once again out-sweated the Godfather at the incongruously formal classical concert venue, with the historical detonation captured on this stellar live album.

As Laurie Stras points out in her book She's So Fine: Femininity in 1960s Music, "Instead of riffing on the theme of lost love, Tina actually stops the music and tells the audience a story of lost love as a spoken monologue, with the inflections and tone of a black preacher in church." Tina adds a personal touch to her story by pausing the music.

"'I'm going to pause the music for a few moments because I want to talk to you about love and pain." If everyone in this house has ever been hurt, I want you to sing together with me right now." The music begins to play again, but she proclaims theatrically that she must pause it again since she hasn't finished talking about love and hurt. The audience erupted.

When this boisterous ensemble surged into Carnegie Hall, Discogs provided an accurate judgment. "At the pinnacle of their international fame, having created their explosive version of Creedence Clearwater Revival's 'Proud Mary' and opening for the Stones on their tour, their visual appeal was equally impressive." The nine-piece outfit ripped through a demonstration of their soul-drenched funk-inflected down and filthy brand of r & b, pushing the rock originals to new heights in their cover versions, unfazed by the formal backdrop of New York's famed concert hall."

This live recording famously captured her remark that she never does anything "nice and easy," but rather "nice and rough," as well as her almost insufferable sexual innuendos with the microphone during "Been Loving You Too Long." Equally telling and eerie was Ike's repeated refrain, which he put into the gentle Otis Redding song he detested. When she sings about being tired and wanting to be free, but her lover's sentiments have grown stronger over time, "I've been loving you a little too long to stop now," the song becomes a classic call-and-response soul pattern. When Tina said, "I can't stop now," Ike's improvised response was, of course, not part of the song: "Cause you ain't ready to die." How lovely.

Tina's partner should have paid closer attention to the lyrics of the other Redding song that Tina had so convincingly adapted here. She grabbed "Respect" away from both Redding and Franklin and made it her own, doing a job that I actually prefer to the already excellent Otis and Aretha versions and at nearly three times their speeds. She merely needed to say the word "respect" louder for her spouse. And very soon.

CHAPTER 5:
PLEASE LET ME GO AND RELEASE ME

During their creative and commercial heyday from the mid-1960s to the mid-1970s, one of Tina Turner's greatest achievements was undoubtedly the sheer tenacity to continue making meaningful musical statements despite emotional and physical trials as well as great personal danger. She steadfastly refused to abandon the person she had become, much to the disgust of those who understood her past, either because she regarded herself as a survivor who could weather any storm or because she was a textbook example of Stockholm syndrome. Was she delusory enough to accept the guy keeping her hostage?

We'll never know what motivated her, and it's not for me to conjecture. The music, on the other hand, kept moving forward in a remarkable example of her trademark against-all-odds optimism, and while we are right to wonder about the psychological roots or contradictions in a hostage's character, we are not entitled to criticize them. In a confident voice, the music she created with her companion speaks for itself, and the music she created following her release from him during her great solo career has now reached the lofty annals of artistic mythology. What goes around comes around, from one eccentric generation to the next.

When attempting to examine the significant life lessons gained by Tina Turner and left for us all to ponder, I recently came across a key comment about resilience that feels like it pertains directly to us. The first observation concerns suffering and its values, and it was made by conceptual artist Barbara Bloom, whose work usually used damaged items or obscured images to highlight the fragility and transient nature of memory. Bloom was referring to the Eastern style known as wabi sabi in her book Broken, which emphasizes the faults or damage, abnormalities or rough patches, of items and even experiences.

Kintsukuroi, which means "to repair with gold," is the technique of fixing shattered or cracked ceramics with gold or silver lacquer and the concept that the thing is more beautiful for having been damaged. This concept entails accepting faults in our experiences and accepting that we are all flawed in some way. Instead than concealing the broken part, wabi sabi attempts to strengthen the damaged sections by emphasizing and even emphasizing the healing process.

Tina Turner's entire approach to learning from and getting beyond her horrific early life, I believe, has much to do with this technique of accepting damage and stressing its possible advantages. Turner is clearly a case of tough patches in life experience, which she used to her advantage both during and after her deliverance from the traumas. Her later songs, I believe, were the gold lacquer she used to repair the fractures in her previous existence.

One issue we frequently debate is how to distinguish between the art produced and the person who generated it. Without discounting the critical role of an individual's autobiographical experience in the creation of their trade, D. H. Lawrence's advice to "never trust the artist, always trust the tale." The proper role of the critic is to save the story from the artist who created it." Yet, while we may divorce her personal narrative from the work she created, we risk overdoing it as appreciators. We're still left wondering about the lyrical content of the songs she functioned as a vehicle for—the message she was conveying in those songs—that is, who exactly is she singing about? Many listeners have noted and commented on the strange fact that Ike's songs frequently repeated the same fundamental issues, ideas, and patterns. Apart from having a narrow range of thoughts, I believe there was also a kind of deep unconscious need to recognize something in which he was complicit. I wouldn't call it guilt because I believe he was incapable of that particular human emotion, but how frequently can the Fool pattern recur without at least some minimal meaning leaking into his addled psyche?

In general, the singer appeared to be taking on the title role; however, I believe it was the insecure writer who felt that diminishment, almost in this order: "A Fool in Love," "Poor Fool," "A Fool for a Fool," "Poor Little Fool," "Foolish," and, of course, "A Fool for You." One has to wonder why this message, combined with the abuse, took so long to reach Tina, but better late than never, I suppose.

She was definitely too preoccupied with performing and recording to take a break for some much-needed contemplation at the moment. And, once again, Ike preferred it this way. Ike Turner, as much of a control freak as any composer or bandleader ever lived, must have felt his grasp on the creative situation diminishing literally day by day as Tina became more and more the headline attraction in his little carnival performance. He eventually became the sideshow geek. Such a strange mixed blessing: his hopes of prosperity coming true were also the very circumstances that threatened to shatter his dream utterly.

In this context, two significant events occurred near the end of 1970. First, after more than a year of performing an explosive version of John Fogerty's "Proud Mary" in their live concerts and on television, Ike decided to bring Tina into the studio to finally let her record her own version, which she completely transformed from the songwriter's earlier delivery and made it all her own. She not only made a brilliant performance that has become synonymous with her name, but she also felt that her version was more authentic to rock and roll than the original, as much as she admired Creedence Clearwater Revival. Tina Turner would virtually be identified as a de facto solo artist by the time Fogerty's Bayou Country record was released, much before she would officially be one. When it was published in early 1971, it quickly soared to become their biggest hit to date, selling over a million copies by May.

Tina received her first Grammy Award for best rhythm and blues vocal performance for this song. Whether or not you believe in the principle of karma (actions and their consequences, both positive and negative), as Tina was and still is, it seemed that whenever Tina needed someone or something to lift her up and move her forward to the next spot on her chess board, they always materialized magically right in front of her.

The grateful original writer of the song, John Fogerty, was effusive in his praise for helping to make his tune the second-biggest single song ever for either of them in Jan Wenner's Rolling Stone piece on

Tina: "Tina Turner doing my 'Proud Mary' is one of the most electrifying images in rock and roll." Thank you, Tina, for catapulting my song into the stratosphere."

"Not to disparage John Fogerty, but Tina Turner certainly put dimensions to 'Proud Mary' that I'm sure he couldn't ever have possibly imagined," Aaron Cohen said to me.

Cohen generally agrees with my assessment of her main strength as a singer. "Empathy, and, of course, sexuality, have been essential to her talents as an interpreter." She surely was an invitation to embrace our most visceral sentiments by being an open channel for them herself. Indeed, she had transformed both the song and herself in the process, explaining in her opening lines about her version, which by then had practically become part of the song's formal lyrics: we're going to start this out doing it nice and easy but then change it up a bit because we never do anything "nice and easy, we always do it nice and rough."

Neither John Corcelli nor I. Corcelli was brief and to the point in evaluating what she did to turn "Proud Mary" from a Creedence Clearwater Revival song into whatever we may call it in her hands, despite not being a singer-songwriter herself. "She took the song and transformed it into her own." In fact, I first heard Ike and Tina Turner's rendition before CCR's. For me, their famous performance on the Ed Sullivan Show remains the ultimate version." Hear, hear.

Aaron Cohen also nails it when he explains what set Tina apart from her many great female peers. "What struck me as unique about Tina Turner was something I hadn't considered until I saw her on an early 1970s (1971 or 1972) episode of The Dick Cavett Show." Her greatest vocal influences, she said, were male vocalists such as Ray Charles. That made me think about her androgyny. Nobody viewing her would think she's attempting to seem manly (like Grace Jones), but the more I thought about it, the more I realized that androgyny comes through in her voice. And I'm curious whether that's why she had such great affinities with male rock artists who also experimented with gender roles, like Mick Jagger and David Bowie."

Again, something unusual in Turner's basic vocal technique tended to make Turner's imprint on the distinctive range of black rock so stylistically crucial for Cohen. "Certainly, her androgyny made a significant contribution to both black and white rock." And because Ike Turner was as good a guitarist as any of the more well-known names in rock, Tina Turner's voice alongside his guitar lines were a big contribution to broadening the parameters of what made black rock what it became." Naturally, the alluringly androgynous Prince comes to mind as a big inheritor of both Ike's guitar and Tina's vibe, merged impossibly into one singular black genius.

The second noteworthy development that year was Ike's decision to finally pursue his long-held desire of creating his own recording studio after recording "Proud Mary" in a prohibitively expensive commercial studio and reaping the tremendous revenues from the song. He'd had it with rehearsing at home in his living room and rushing through sessions at places that were booked by the hour. His fantasy, or, more precisely, delusion, was that he could establish a personal hit factory in his own studio, a la Phil Spector, whom he both admired and detested.

He intended to rename it Bolic Sound Studio, a play on his wife's maiden name in an ironic nod to the source of his creative and financial freedom. He could have just as well named it Bullock Studio: that would have been the most suitable way to spend the vast sums of money she was bringing in and that he was preparing to put in a small building on La Brea, just a few minutes away from his View Park Hills location. It had been totally refurbished, renovated, soundproofed, and outfitted with what he thought he deserved: cutting-edge technology, including an over $100,000 control board. This, he thought, was a wise investment (pun intended), because he firmly, if delusively, felt that new hits would soon pour out of the site.
He also gave himself the luxury of two complete and distinct sound studios in the building, including a large room that he would rent out to big-name stars he thought deserving. It was eventually used on several occasions by none other than Frank Zappa, so it must have been technically proficient. Given their polar opposite musical interests and temperaments, that must have been an unusual business

partnership to say the least. Zappa recorded some amazing albums in Bolic Sound, including his famous hit Apostrophe, and Tina even did some backup vocals on his Overnite Sensation album.

Ike also created a smaller studio for his own personal use, which he used to record his now-famous protégée Tina. He even built a separate sanctuary (or party room) behind a completely sealed-off security vault door, as he became increasingly worried about privacy and security. His control obsessions dictated that he build a complex system of closed-circuit video cameras throughout the house for both security and paranoia. Naturally, Ike retained a small armory of weaponry, both pistols and machine guns, cleverly positioned here and there.

This combination did not bode well, considering the mountains of cocaine he could now indulge in secretly, as well as his already well-documented terrible husband skills and frequent volcanic rages. Fortunately for the studio's nominal name, push never came to shove and shoot, though after Tina managed to free herself from his control and file for divorce (still five years away at this point), her car was frequently found torched, and bullets were frequently fired into her independent home away from home.

The year 1971 was shaping up to be one of his and their most successful yet, with their latest Revue album, What You Hear Is What You Get, peaking at number 25 on the charts in the summer. Both were also included in the film documentary Soul to Soul, which was shot in Ghana, Africa, to commemorate the country's 40th anniversary of independence, and both sang a song in the Milos Forman film Taking Off.

The first high-profile public disclosure of the couple's marital problems and Ike's clear mental problems in the still-stunning Ben Fong-Torres Rolling Stone cover story on October 14, 1971 was a major setback for this year. Even if he was humiliated by all the public attention this brought, for the first time revealing Tina's life with Ike, and even if he was angry, he didn't seem to have the typical human gene for shame. He just proceeded further up Coke Mountain, as if it were his personal Everest, and counted his larger and larger acres of cash.

That article may have contributed in some small way to him reining in his proclivities (the Tina violence, not the coke romance), as well as providing Tina with the strength of public awareness and the support system she'd need when she eventually made her escape from the Ike cult. But, as the money flowed in and the adoration for his now-megastar wife peaked, his own popularity as the leader of a once-thriving Revue began to dwindle. Their next album, Nuff Said, the first produced by his "hit factory," failed to make the Top 100, and the next single, "Up in Heah," only managed to reach number 83, while a second factory-produced album, Feel Good, ranked even lower.

Things were not going as planned for the black Spector. Tina had definitely learned by then that times were changing and that musical styles and tastes were developing (as were her own), but she also noted that her husband's music style and stage presentation never changed. It was basically the same one he'd been doing since the end of the 1950s when she first approached his stage. Tina was also inspired by the feminist movement and the concept of women's liberation, however she thought it amusing that most women were attempting to be emancipated from housekeeping, whilst she was merely attempting to survive.

A hot-blooded dance song and album reflecting her family's southern origins in Tennessee would emerge, albeit a little late, and it was such an ironic and contradictory hit. In the fall of 1973, the aforementioned "Nutbush City Limits" peaked at number 22 on the pop charts. It was the couple's final Top 30 hit together, and her husband couldn't help but notice that it was all about her childhood roots and personal progress.

Tina also wrote a song identical to the title track for the same album, "Club Manhattan," about the place where she met Ike, as well as a supercharged song about her beginnings with him: "Over in E. In St. Louis, there's a swingin' little club called Manhattan, and the band on that stage are kings of rhythm," in addition to several other first-time-ever self-written songs: "Daily Bread," "Help Him" (a strange Tammy Wynette-clone), and one that has a distinctly gospel feeling, although it's gospel funk to be sure: "That's My Purpose." But I was sent here to adore you, and that's my purpose," she chirped, almost seriously.

Personally, I interpret that song's message as meaning she's here to love all of us, not just "him." Meanwhile, Ike's own strange tune for the album also contained a not-so-subtle and somewhat ominous message to his partner: "Get It Out of Your Mind." But for me, one of the most salient aspects of a jaunty little rocker like "Nutbush City Limits" is that the little town in question was not incorporated by the In a strange sense, Nutbush was everywhere she went, and so she was still living in Nutbush, even in Europe, because she couldn't really leave it, and as a thirty-four-year-old worldly woman rather than the innocent rural girl, she also realized the time was past ripe for a significant shift. She had, however, finally arrived at the actual municipal limits and borderline between Anna Mae Bullock and Tina Turner.

Aaron Cohen's biggest accomplishment as a musician was completely utilizing the instrument she was born with. "Her voice on those late-'60s/early '70s Ike & Tina Turner recordings, as well as her dynamic stage presence, would be my favorite among her accomplishments." But I can also see how those who have been victims of personal hardships see her as an important role model." True, she's an all-purpose goddess in that regard, as well as absolutely unlimited. Someone up there likes me, she must have been saying all the time. No matter how terrible things were, they always got better. The office of record producer Robert Stigwood called them to check about her availability for a film he was helping to finance for eccentric British director Ken Russell, known for films such as The Devils and Women in Love. The film was a cinematic adaptation of The Who's bombastic rock opera Tommy from 1969, a song she had heard of but never truly heard.

It had an all-star cast: Elton John, Eric Clapton, the Who, Oliver Reed, Jack Nicholson, Ann-Margaret as Tommy's mother, and Tina Turner if she wanted to play the Acid Queen. There is no mention of Ike. Filming in London was a lot of fun, and it gave her the opportunity to reunite with her old Las Vegas companion Ann-

Margaret, who then asked her to stay on after the production was finished to collaborate with her on her newest television musical spectacular. Their duets on "Nutbush City Limits," "Honky Tonk Women," and "Proud Mary" were also big hits on television.

Meanwhile, back in his toxic Bolic studios (which by then should have been termed hyperbole), Ike had recently increased his capacity from twenty-four to thirty-two tracks, maybe in the aim of capturing some of Spector's superb overdubs on his own. But it only allowed him to have way too many different versions of songs without knowing how to sort through all of his coke-addled attempts.

When someone shoves hot coffee in your face, it becomes immediately evident (if it wasn't already) that he didn't love Tina for herself but was instead preoccupied with keeping control of her and, by extension, with the comfortable creative lifestyle she enabled. These mid-career discs would be ideal for any young individual looking for a crash education in their dynamic allure. However, as popular as they were, it was never lost on Ike that their most successful and adored songs and albums were frequently those that he did not wholly write or produce. That made the big boss man even more difficult to get along with, assuming that was even possible given his pathology.

Nuff Said and Feel Good, both released on United Artists in 1972, immediately solidified their excellent rhythm, but the vibe had begun to wear a bit thin by this point, as had their relationship, which had never been anything but unstable from the outset. They were mostly together in name only by that point. Tina Turns the Country On, her one-of-a-kind (if slightly strange) solo effort from 1974, was a clear indicator that she was more than ready to move on without Ike.

Finally, she'd broken out on her own, at least musically, with her unusual but charming country-flavored CD of cover songs, which had to be rewarding on some level. It didn't exactly turn the country on, being largely a lame cash grab on Ike's part, but most listeners were impressed by her creative adaptability and complete lack of professional skill. People loved her sincerity and perseverance even when she failed.

Her mutability as an artist, according to John Corcelli, is what makes her so unique. "Clearly, Turner made the perhaps unexpected transition from R&B to Rock and then to Pop, but my guess is that she also brought everything from those earlier musical worlds forward with her into Pop as an art form." And she accomplished this extraordinary feat without not compromising anything along the way: she remained true to herself regardless of the style she adopted. She also made significant contributions to the stylistic growth of each genre she touched."

Aaron Cohen believes that her determination and ardent dedication to sheer hard work ultimately triumphed over any minor vocal restrictions she may have had. "Tina Turner didn't have Aretha Franklin's range or Mavis Staples' family lineage, but she worked incredibly hard to make the most of the voice she had." And she brought a physicality and theatricality to her performances that few of her contemporaries, regardless of gender or race, possessed. She also made rougher vocal traits fit into the soul era (like Etta James did), but I can't imagine Mary Wells or Tammi Terrell ever doing that. Tina's actions most certainly contributed to Bettye LaVette's later reemergence."

I agree, and I believe she paved the way for a niche that could accept a funky artist as raw as Betty Mabry-Davis, not to mention certain female rappers. One of the qualities that most intrigued John Corcelli was her incredible creative versatility. "I believe Tina's most significant artistic achievement has been her ability to transcend categories entirely." Turner, in fact, has firmly earned her place in popular music by never making aesthetic compromises. She has also shaped her own career, rather than having it shaped by her handlers or record executives. We must recall that Ike had always attempted to 'manage' her artistic career from the beginning. She ultimately gained complete charge of her own repertoire after breaking away from his grasp, and she made much better and higher quality creative musical selections. Turner's willingness to take artistic risks has resulted in a respectable and fulfilling discography for his admirers. "After all, only Tina Turner could have sung 'What's Love Got to Do with It?'"

But, perhaps unsurprisingly, it took Tina a while to fully come into herself and find her own footing once she attempted to present herself as a truly solo artist (on two albums while still with the Revue band) and another two follow-up solo albums while caught in a strange kind of transitional period of stylistic searching.

As I already stated, her first two efforts were pretty unusual, bordering on kitschy. Tina Turns the Country On! In any case, and to be as charitable as possible, Tina Turns the Country On! is a slightly strange pastiche of crooked western melodies on which she appears drastically out of place, owing to the fact that she is. And Acid Queen (1975) is a novelty send-up to complement her then-recent acting role in the Who's campy Ken Russell film, an album for which she deserves credit just for maintaining a straight face throughout. It's a good selection of hard rockers for her to cover, but it's accompanied by a second side dish of more terrible late Ike compositions.

TINA TURNS ON THE COUNTRY! UNION OF ARTISTS RECORDS

It was released in 1974. Tom Thacker was in charge of the production. Joe Lamno on bass; Michael Bolts on drums; Mark Creamer on guitars; Glen Hardin on keyboard; J. Terrance Lane, percussion; D. Minnis, steel guitar; Tom Scott, saxophone. John Horton, Fred Borkgren, Steve Waldman, and D. B. Johnson was the engineer. Duration: 33:49 (which feels like an eternity).

Bayou Song (P. J. Morse) 3:22 / Help Me Make It Through the Night (Kris Kristofferson) 2:48 / Tonight I'll Be Staying Here With You (Bob Dylan) 2:58 / If You Love Me (John Rostill) 3:00 / Don't Talk Now (James Taylor) 2:58 / Long Long Time (Gary White) 4:42

Don't get me wrong here. If you've gotten this far in the book. You already know how much I admire this artist. However, everyone makes mistakes, and this was hers—or, rather, theirs, as it was her husband's idea: a somewhat cynical attempt to broaden their fan base by leveraging his major commodity: her. But what about the country? True, I'm not a big fan, but I know good country when I hear it (Kitty Wells, Patsy Cline, Tammy Wynette, June Carter, and

Dolly Parton before she became a mainstream star), and this isn't it. They even tried to describe it as country rhythm and blues, which is a blatant contradiction in terms.

Even if your typically popular rhythm and blues is experiencing a sales slowdown, it was a risky bet as your first solo debut album. Despite this, Tina received a Grammy nomination for best rhythm-and-blues female vocal performance in 1974, which still baffles me to this day. Of course, this record did not do well and was never published on CD. Count your blessings, perhaps, but I completely see why Tina completists would want it in their collection, as I have a healthy compulsive tendency myself.

It should also not be confused with a slew of other odd Ike attempts to cash in, even after she'd left him, such as Tina Turner Sings Country, Soul Deep, Country My Way, Good Hearted Woman, Country in My Soul, Stand by Your Man (really!), Country Classics, You Ain't Woman Enough to Take My Man (poor Tammy!), and The Country Side of Tina Turner, all of which represented Ike's persistence,

(UNITED ARTISTS RECORDS) ACID QUEEN

Denny Diante and Spencer Proffer produced. It was released in 1975. Tina Turner (vocals), Ike Turner (arranger), Ed Greene (drums), Henry Davis (bass), Ray Parker (guitar), Spence Proffer (guitar), Jerry Peters (keyboards), Joe Clayton (congas), Alan Lindgren (synthesizer), Sid Sharp (strings), Julia Waters, Kim Carnes, Maxine Waters (vocals), Denny Diante (percussion), Ray Milano (recording and mixing). The video lasts 35:29 minutes.

Under My Thumb (Mick Jagger, Keith Richards) 3:22 / Let's Spend the Night Together (Mick Jagger, Keith Richards) 2:54 / Acid Queen (Pete Townshend) 3:01 / I Can See for Miles (Pete Townshend) 2:54 / Whole Lotta Love (Willie Dixon) 5:24 / Baby Get It On (Ike Turner) 5:34 / Bootsy White

At the very least, it isn't country and western (sorry, Dolly). Although it was another clear attempt to capitalize on her frenetic cinematic Tommy turn (but why should we really hold it against her?), it had all the makings of something heavy load. I wish they had stuck to all Townshend material instead of mixing and matching classic hard rock anthems and then diluting it all with a side dish of outdated Ike raunch odes past their prime. "Bootsy Whitelaw," his dedication to a jazz trombone great who influenced him early in his career, is an unusual theme for an acid queen operetta. I would have liked her to perform not only Tommy material (which would have been too clichéd), but also some other Who masterpieces, such as "Happy Jack" (a personal fave) or "A Quick One While He's Away."

"Her rock myth reconfirmed cinematically, Tina quickly turns out two from the Who (only fair), two from the Stones (who else?) and one from Led Zep ("Whole Lotta Love" is brilliant)," wrote Robert Christgau in his Rock Albums of the Seventies. The singing practically doesn't matter with bass lines stolen full from the originals. And what mythically rocks the hardest? Ike's ingeniously titled 'Baby Get It On.'" The latter song, which is almost (but not quite) as disco inspired as Tina's next two genuinely solo albums, was the pair's last reasonably successful rhythm-and-blues single together.

1974-1975 was another banner year for the troubled partnership, as they descended into their inevitable downward spiral—for a variety of reasons. During those years, there was one more fantastic live record, a double album called The World of Ike and Tina Turner! Let Me Touch Your Mind, also from United Artists, won a Grammy Award for best album package, as well as Ike Turner Presents the Family Vibes—Strange Fruit, with vaguely eclectic but overused synthesizers by Ike in one of his sinister pseudo psychedelic side projects with his original Rhythm Kings band in tow.

In 1974, they added two similarly significant and reputable additions to their portfolio. The Gospel According to Ike and Tina Turner, their nineteenth studio album, features fresh arrangements of traditional gospel tunes (something every secular blues/soul musician eventually does), but is unduly reliant on Ike's new synthesizer fixation. Nonetheless, it was nominated for a Grammy in the gospel category in 1975! Finally (nearly) came Sweet Rhode Island Red, their final studio effort before splitting up, which included several new Tina songs as well as versions of well-known Stevie Wonder songs.

The fact that he released almost as many albums of her music after she left him as he did when they were together, mostly using alternate takes, unreleased songs, B-side rejects, or literally anything else containing her voice that was gathering dust in his Bolic Studio vaults, is one of the reasons I tend to use the word "finally" in italics (or certainly tongue in cheek when it comes to Ike).

His fixation with regularly recording her would pay off for him for decades to come, even if the releases were less than up to their usual high standards by then. He couldn't tell the difference without her around, and moreover, she was his prized thoroughbred champion, or so he believed, and he wasn't about to let anything she said go to waste. According to my reckoning, thirty vault recordings on various labels, many of them European, made their way into the world following her dramatic comeback without him.

If he could, he would have released her while she was reading from the phone book. Delilah's Power, an album released after her departure

(With the exception of the title song, which was already a single from two years prior, when they were traveling in Europe), was published one year after she escaped him, in 1976, in order for him to capitalize on his soon-to-be ex-wife's Midas touch. Ike was spending more time at Bolic Sound than he was with Tina and their children at their Inglewood home at the time. Tina, on the other hand, had turned within to find solace after being introduced to the contemplative teachings of Buddhism and chanting.

In July 1976, Ike planned to sign a five-year contract with a new record label, Cream Records, for a reported annual salary of $150,000. The contract had a significant "personal" condition that required Ike to sign the contract within four days, tying Tina to Ike for at least another five years. She couldn't go on for another five minutes. The Ike and Tina Turner Revue took an aircraft to Dallas on

July 2, 1976, to perform at the Dallas Statler Hilton. The two became involved in a disagreement on the plane, which culminated in a violent fight in their limousine.

The two gave opposing narratives of what happened that day. Ike accused Tina of being inattentive in helping him with a nosebleed caused by chronic cocaine usage, and his bizarre answer was to do even more cocaine. Tina claimed Ike was irritated because she was eating chocolates while dressed completely in white, prompting Like to slap and strike her. The couple did agree on one point: Ike had been awake for five days straight on a cocaine binge.

Tina recalls fighting back for the first time after Ike's strike, clawing and kicking him. Both Ike and Tina were bleeding by the time they got to the hotel, according to Ike, who claimed to a musician association buddy that the two "went around like prizefighters for a while." Ike retired on a sofa after heading up to their suite. Tina grabbed a few toiletries, covered herself, and fled through the back of the motel, racing over an active motorway before stopping at a nearby Ramada Inn.

She stated that she eventually hid out at many friends' homes for a period of time, insisting on helping them with household tasks and obligations despite their attempts to stop her. In Trouble Girls, Christian Wright captured her arrogant and meek personality perfectly. "Tina Turner was a star, but she was never a diva." When her roommates told her to stop cleaning because the cleaner would do it, she persisted since she needed to pay her rent. She didn't think less of herself for it because it helped her survive, she claimed. She was pleased with herself."

Tina Turner filed for divorce on July 27, 1976, citing irreconcilable differences. It's about time. Ike and Tina fought in divorce court for a year, disputing over money and property. Tina decided to stop pursuing any financial earnings, including an apartment complex in Anaheim, California, and another apartment elsewhere, in late 1977, telling her lawyer that her freedom "was much more important." Tina also agreed to keep only her stage name, which came in handy for her upcoming reincarnation.

The divorce processes were completed in November 1977, and the divorce was finalized in March 1978. With the self-awareness of a clam, it never dawned on Ike that it wasn't the fault or shortcoming of others around him for "abandoning" him all the time, but rather the effect of his being such a miserable human being. That would have needed far too much introspection.

"Tumultuous: it's an interesting word to choose in considering Turner's artistic endeavors in music and movies," John Corcelli told me. "That said, she is definitely an artist who has taken a lot of personal struggle and, as blues artists often did, expressed her pain through her music." So, from that standpoint, it works. Nonetheless, I believe Turner has elevated herself to her audience as an important way of recuperation. Her time with Ike was obviously unpleasant, but her unwavering pursuit of her own identity, as best heard in all of her work, has been a complete confirmation of who she is, both as an artist, a woman, and a person."

Indeed, analyzing Ike Turner's vital yet disturbing role has always been difficult. It is tempered, according to Corcelli, by a few essential and incontrovertible facts. "On a strictly musical level, Ike has earned his place in music history as one of the founders of sound': the Gospel/funk/Pop blend that made the Ike & Tina Turner Revue such a rousing success." The fact that he mistreated Tina has deservedly tarnished his personal reputation, but I believe it is inappropriate to view his total contribution to music through the lens of domestic abuse.``

True, he leaves a troublesome legacy, and, like many artists, his work is best examined apart from his character or personality. Ironically, it frequently amazes me that it was his ex-partner's caustic attitude and challenging mentality that encouraged or provoked him to pursue a solo career in the first place. So, in some ways (and strangely), his personal psychological issues made just as significant, if unintentional, a contribution to our collective cultural history as his original musical combination of ideas did.

In terms of what was about to happen to each of the ex-partners, I was reminded of an obscure quote from Robert Louis Stevenson in an elegy he wrote shortly before writing the aptly titled Strange Case of Jekyll and Hyde, an observation that perfectly applies to the Ike and Tina situation: "Sooner or later, everyone sits down to a banquet of consequences."

Tina deserved to be revived in her own image

Karma is a strange thing, except when it isn't. Some exotic deliverance had appeared out of nowhere—and from an unexpected and humorous source considering her circumstances. Late in 1974, she received a gift of introspective and restorative energy that would serve her well later in life. It would be another two years before her turbulent relationship with the plainly atrociously abusive husband fate had placed by her side came to a head. That same psycho-husband, in fact, brought an attractive Jewish woman home and introduced her to Tina.

She assumed it was just another in his never-ending procession of secretaries, assistants, managers, and flitting Ikettes, but this one was different, and she didn't survive long in the fold either. Valerie Bishop, on the other hand, stayed only long enough to expose the depressed vocalist to Nichiren Shoshu Buddhism, a distinct brand of meditational practice combining contemplative breath techniques of chanting. As previously said, it would have long-term consequences for her that persist to this day.

This technique was supposedly validated for her by Jackie Stanton, a close friend who was a dancer, and incorporated shakubuku as the initial level of its gentle and calming lessons. Bishop left her with a book, some beads for meditation, and the main chant of this particular sect, which was formed by a thirteenth-century radical Buddhist master, Nichiren, as part of the Mahayana school during the Kamakura period.

This teaching is based on the idea that everyone possesses the innate enlightened state known as Buddha-nature, or awakened awareness, but it is dormant and generally concealed by limited frameworks such as identity and ego, and it is certainly clouded by personal sufferings, leading to fear, confusion, and inhibition. Apart from faith in the Lotus Sutra, a key philosophical text in the Buddhist canon, its most visible tenet is the mind-calming practice of chanting: in this case, the chanting of nam-myo-ho-renge-kyo, which essentially means an expression of homage to the truth in the sutra teachings as exemplified by Nichiren himself, something of a radical and prophetic figure historically.

Tina began chanting (while still living with Ike) as a way to calm her distressed mind, but she soon became interested in the meditative means of subduing illusory projections that might allow a person to transcend one's current limited condition, in her case the posttrauma of victimhood. She practiced this practice when her abusive caretaker was not there, and she also acquired a butsudan, a little cabinet or reliquary containing symbolic requirements such as candles, water, incense, and scripture rolls, comparable to the Western concept of an altar. This was all absent from the concept of worship, because Buddhism had no inherent deity other than a form of divine consciousness linked with cleansed human awareness.

Her husband, who was not known for his depth of philosophical or spiritual knowledge, responded with fear and disgust, asking that she remove her shrine cabinet and stop muttering. He was most certainly misinterpreting things, as he often did, and in his self-saturated narcotic haze sensed a nonexistent voodoo element to the whole episode, which could not be explained away. The beauty of her new exercise, however, was that it required no outward displays of activity and could be carried out silently and internally as a technique of controlling her own supposed constraints.

When she spoke to Minerva Lee for Lotus Happiness magazine in 2018, she stressed the ability of what she called the miracle of daimoku to enhance life, which she had witnessed directly. She remembered a friend telling her that Buddhism would not only transform her life but, in her instance, literally save her life. So she continued her meditation practice, especially her chanting, up to three hours a day, even in the midst of her continual violent abuse by Ike, in an obvious attempt to cure trauma in the present moment, while it was still happening.

In the middle of these emotional transformations, just prior to her divorce, the film Tommy was released in early 1975, much to the surprise of critics but much to the delight of pop music enthusiasts. It did, however, earn Ann-Margaret an Academy Award nod for her performance as Tommy's mother, particularly in the famed baked beans sequence. Melody Maker, a music magazine rather than a film magazine, lost its marbles and dubbed it a work of art while also praising Ann-Margaret and Turner's strange performances. It has to do with the medicines the audience had taken prior to watching.

The Revue's and its brilliant duet's hit singles had pretty much dried up by this point, with "Baby Get It On" reaching number 88 to a deafening commercial silence. Basically, hardly one wanted to hook up with the couple anymore. Tina tried to leave him twice, once for a few days, once for a few weeks, and finally, on July 4, 1976, during a Bicentennial celebration week in Dallas, where they were supposed to perform, she lulled him to sleep and disappeared into the night. She stayed at the home of their joint attorney, whom she trusted, until she realized that no one working for Ike could be trusted.

She moved into the Lookout Mountain home of a girlfriend, the sister of jazz artist Wayne Shorter. Then she went around like a fugitive from mafia hit men, holding a.38-caliber handgun in her purse. She underlined that there would be no going back after one final meeting in a car with his thuggish attorneys. Ike then sent her two children, as well as his own two, to live with her. She had to look after them as well as repay promoters for bailing off the final Revue tour, so she took whatever little gig she could get, especially the tried-and-true cabaret circuit, where loads of people were ready to see her with or without her insane mentor.

She wisely concluded that her living her life itself was more essential than any of the objects in that life, having opted to give up all claims on creative or economic rights and merely wishing to start over from fresh. She received BMI royalties for some of her own songs, then formed her own band, a real rock band this time, and released her first post-Ike solo record, Rough, which didn't exactly set the world on fire. But it was only her first salvo.

Tina was evidently openly sharing her delight in doing what most people take for granted: making all of her own decisions, big and little. When the divorce was finalized, she cut her hair and went shopping, despite the fact that she had no money. She made it through, though, and she was finally having fun. It was a liberation that is difficult to convey or comprehend until you have experienced some type of bondage.

"It was a full sixteen years of abuse—and two years of chanting—before Tina left Ike forever in 1976," Lee wrote in Lotus Happiness. What is the meaning of the four-word Buddhist chant that helped her? "'Nam' means devotion, 'Myo' means mystic, 'Ho' means law, 'Renge' means lotus blossom, and 'Kyo' means sutra (teaching)." It is not extremely scholarly, intellectually difficult, or philosophical, yet it is profound and focuses primarily on compassion for all suffering fellow sentient creatures. This teaching emphasizes that both sorrow and joy are facts of life, and that both can be intensified or diminished by our own reactions to anything we meet.

"When I first started chanting is also when I started using my head, I started thinking—I'm not going to kill myself, there's nothing here for me," Tina explained to Lee. This person has no idea that I am assisting him, that I have attempted to be good and friendly to him. I didn't have anyone, no foundation in life, so I had to forge my own path. Have done so since the beginning. I had to go out into the world and grow up."

It was a moving event for her to reflect on that transformative era in her life. "I gradually began to feel like myself again." And now, forty-five years of chanting have opened a door within me, changing my life for the better. I've left a substantial body of work as a rock vocalist, and I've made it quite apparent that it was all due to my spiritual practice."

She has also demonstrated a daring ability to share her personal problems with the entire world, allowing the rest of us to do the same. Her new calm, tranquil, and considerably loser attitude toward life even allowed her to perform downright foolish undertakings for the sake of amusement. Everyone around her could see the impact of her shift of focus away from her abuser and toward herself and her inner nature, except for the main source of her pain, of course.

In 1978, she had a great time working on Robert Stigwood's cheerful but shapeless cinematic take on the Beatles' Sergeant Pepper motifs, in which he attempted to replicate his Tommy triumph but fell short. Critics were unimpressed with the film, but they were constantly moved by Tina's presence on screen, regardless of what she was doing. Her much more comfortable demeanor looked to be reflected in the camera as well.

She was eager to take on new challenges, even if some of them would necessitate some humility and patience until she had paid her solitary dues. That was fine with her because she had already overpaid her dues previous to her solo career and knew she deserved some pay-back sooner or later. But her retaliation was already well on its way.

CHAPTER 6:
NIGHTS OF NICHIREN

We've all been through transitional periods in our lives, when we're in between those unmistakable landmarks that bring meaning and stability. Naturally, few of us have experienced the level of extreme instability that Tina Turner has, or have had to weather the storm that appears to be generated by decisions we made early on and those we felt forced to make later on. This is the point in her story when she went on a hazy voyage into no-man's land, with no man to guide her as there had been since she was sixteen. She may have been lost without a map, but she was not lost without a compass.

When we are caught in a kind of interim zone of interrupted choices, we might best study how we got here while attempting to figure out where to go next. That same internal and intuitive compass that had led her here would lead her there, whatever that was. She was already counting her blessings for escaping from an unusual form of creative and personal prison, but she'd soon be able to appraise the vast possibilities that liberation entailed.

Several music critics, musicians, historians, and journalists I spoke with concerning her artistic and cultural contributions had quite varied, yet parallel, perspectives on her continuous trajectory. It's a path I recognize as a cadence and cascade sequence. Cadence is a pattern or rhythm that we all follow whether we realize it or not, whereas cascade is a set of processes that unfold over time and usually become evident only in retrospect. In reality, it is very clear. Without a big label other than modest Capitol/EMI affiliates (at least her British fan base remained active), she was also close with Festival Records in Australia, where she had a cult following (but the positive sort of cult this time). With the decade nearing to an end, 1979 found her completely disoriented until fate intervened in the most unexpected of ways. Olivia Newton-John, fresh off her Grease hit, wanted Tina to appear in one of her popular television specials, and John's manager, Lee Kramer, had been recommended to Tina by one of her dancers and close friends. He was looking for new talent to promote, she explained.

Tina wasn't quite new, but she was certainly exciting. Lee Kramer met a young Australian management guru named Roger Davies through Olivia Newton-John, and the two of them agreed to fly to San Francisco late that fall to see her stage show at the Fairmont Hotel, where they caught her on her final night. She was struggling to make a serious comeback at this point, and her name had gone slightly off the public's radar.

The daring agent Lee Kramer had to explain to his new partner Roger Davies that, while Tina Turner was still alive and performing, her present incarnation was not a true comeback because it did not involve the Revue or her mentor. It was really much more exhilarating for those very reasons, and it felt more like an emergence from a dark closet. It was all up to her now.

She was definitely looking for a new creative path, which can take some time, and she wasn't unduly sad that the spotlight hadn't returned to her. "Once you've experienced a type of bondage and then gotten free, you really learn what being free is all about, and it's just being comfortable with yourself," she said in Off the Record by Joe Smith. So I didn't place any weight on not having an immediate hit record or not being as visible. I was fine where I was, I kept an eye on myself, it was study time after Ike."

This was a wise statement from someone who had become renowned so quickly that she had not pursued any further schooling after high school. As a result, instead of furthering her formal education, she had become a student of herself. She was also ready to graduate, not just from the hard knocks school, but with a master's degree in triumph.

Her first two sincere attempts at a post-Ike persona, 1978's Rough and 1979's Love Explosion, suffered with the same flaws as her country album and caustic monarch outing. In the second occasion, it was her daring but ill-advised foray into pseudo-disco dance music, which was neither a good fit for her dancing talent nor her vintage voice. Of course, she wasn't alone in trying new styles (as many great artists do), and sometimes it works, sometimes it doesn't. The exceptional ones, on the other hand, never stop exploring. So she continued to chant.

(UNITED ARTISTS RECORDS) ROUGH

Bob Monaco, Jill Harris, and Conway Recording Studios produced the album. It was released in 1978. Personnel include Rick Kellis on horns, Ken Moore on piano, Airto Moreria on percussion, Dennis Belfield on bass, Michael Boddicker on synthesizer, Peter Bunetta on drums, Al Ciner on acoustic guitar, Denise Echols and Venetta Fields on vocals, Bill Oz on harmonica, Ron Stockert on clavinet, Willie Smith on organ, and Gerald Lee on strings. The video lasts 41:15 minutes.

4:05 / The Bitch Is Back (Elton John and Bernie Taupin) 3:30 / Viva La Money (Allen Toussaint) 3:14 / Funny How Time Slips Away (Willie Nelson) 4:08 / Root Toot Undisputable (Gary Jackson) 4:29 / Fire Down Below (Bob Seger) 3:13 /

On the bright side, it wasn't labeled Nice and Rough. She was also free to make her own mistakes by this point, rather than being guided to them by an impresario who preyed on her skills. The disadvantage? Disco was the final resting place for rhythm and blues, soul, and funk. Instead, she is led down a perilous path by new producers who prey on her gifts and by the peculiar social party wavelength of the times. So it is. However, the forced marriage of blues and disco produces an odd result here, as does the odd mix of song selections, as if handpicked by a schizoid club management or mad deejay.

Her third solo album had three distributors, presumably in keeping with the album's multiphrenic tracks. When the composers picked are as diverse as Elton John, Willie Nelson, Willie Dixon, Bob Seger, Hal David, and the ever-saccharine Dan Hill, you know disaster is on the way. That's a brain salad for you. And, of course, Bernie Taupin's light mocking of his longtime creative collaborator Elton John's personality (The Bitch is Back) works well when delivered by Elton but not so well when delivered by Tina's character.

This is also her first solo record with no involvement from Ike, so that partially excuses it. But, like Acid Queen before it, it failed to chart or gain any certifications, selling fairly poorly, and despite being converted to CD in the 1990s, it is currently out of print—perhaps a blessing in disguise. Surprisingly, it arrived just as two important musical events occurred at the same time: Elvis Presley's death and the rise of punk. Rough and Love Explosion, however, are happily snuggled in the frigid embrace of disco.

RECORDED IN EUROPE, LOVE EXPLOSION (LIBERTY RECORDS).

Alec Constandinos directed the film. It was released in 1979. Tina Turner (vocals), Jean-Claude Chavanat (guitar), Tony Bonfils (bass), Bernard Arcadio (keyboards), Andre Ceccarelli (drums), Manu Roche (percussion), George Young, Lawrence Feldman, Michael Brecker (tenor saxophones), Lew Del Gatto (baritone), Pat Haling (strings), George Rodi (synthesizer). Mike Ross-Trevor, Scott Litt, Geoff Calver, and Peter Kelsey were the engineers. Raymond Knehnestky composed the music. Peter Kelsey reworked the track at Trident Studios in London. The video lasts 36:05.

5:55 / Fool for Your Love (Leo Sayer, Michael Omartian) 3:24 / Sunset on Sunset (Billy Livsey, David Courtney, Richard Niles) 3:35 / Music Keeps Me Dancing' (Lenny Macaluso, Pat Summerson) 3:49 / I See Home (Allee Willis, David Lasley) 5:19

Okay, we won't hold it against her that she permitted the use of synthesizers for anesthetic purposes; after all, by the late 1970s, practically everyone was doing so. It's also quite acceptable to take artistic license and fall head over heels with Alec Constandinos, a serious top dance producer in France. It's even fine to give it the completely disco-flavored title of Love Explosion and have Tina beaming in her glossy vinyl jumpsuit (who could complain about that?), and who knows, it could all have worked as an end-of-the-decade experiment in the dominant musical style of the moment. But it didn't, even with the familiarly themed "Fool for Your Love" on it.

It achieved little success on both European and American charts, but it wasn't certified, and all of her labels decided to cut ways with her in dismay. The corporate types (this was her final album for EMI and United Artists) don't appear to have realized that the problem wasn't so much Tina as it was their decision to allow her to go on a blind date with synth-disco in the first place.

The two non-dance tunes were promising soulful ballads, one a beautiful one initially performed by Dusty Springfield ten years earlier, but sandwiching them with the thump thump of the disco atmosphere killed the overall venture. When this delectable delicacy was unwrapped, huge changes were afoot in the music industry once more. One of them would go on to become the most significant musical style of the late twentieth century: the introduction of rap and its consequential cousin, hiphop, in the form of Sugarland Express and their 1979 breakthrough single "Rappers Delight."

Love Explosion, like her last effort Rough, did not ignite or explode, and it is now, mercifully, out of print. Love Explosion died quietly in a polished universe where the urgent grit of rap had yet to enter. The good news was that Tina's resurrection was waiting in the wings, patiently ticking away like a nuclear fission blast, following this publication and after a five-year break. Tina's musical transition from rhythm and blues, soul, funk, and rock to pop was almost as significant in terms of industry effect as punk or rap, but in a completely opposite direction.

In retrospect, we all have some common and some divergent viewpoints on the tremendously crazy trip known as the 1980s, which was, in many respects, the polar antithesis of the 1960s while also being an unanticipated yet logical extension of that decade. These two decades, according to Aaron Cohen, were more than just opposing extremes of emancipation and tyranny; they were almost warped funhouse mirror reflections. "I believe that in many respects, the conservative 1980s required a persona that was anything but. I'm also not sure what was going on in the women's movement at the time, but she would have been a powerful advocate for empowerment at a critical juncture. She also understood mediums such as video better than many of her counterparts from earlier decades."

In many ways, the 1980s were an even better decade for Tina's unique attitude than the 1960s, if that's even conceivable.

Roger Davies would be Karma Incorporated, both from the perspective of the newly solo Tina Turner and from ours as a global audience poised to witness her amazing reincarnation. Davies and Kramer's first contact with her post-Ike presence in San Francisco was a surprising surprise, as Davies related to Kurt Loder in what I commonly refer to as her early testimonial. "We went into the Fairmont Hotel, the Venetian Room, this big room with chandeliers and tuxedoed people, and I thought, this can't be the right room." But then Tina came on and blew me away with her intensity. People were standing on tables, and the chandeliers shook."

Kramer was equally taken aback, despite the fact that he felt he knew what to expect from the newcomer. Both he and Davies enthusiastically agreed to take her on, with the main challenge being how to dramatically revamp her act and presentation in order to lift her out of what they accurately described as "cabaret purgatory." As usual with Turner, the unexpected opportunity arose from the most unlikely of places: an offer for her performing services for a $150,000 deal to perform in South Africa, which was still segregated, for a five-week tour.

This was obviously risky for an artist of color and notoriety who had grown up in a segregated part of America, but she was assured that all the venues would be integrated, and yes, ever the optimist no matter what the odd circumstances, she firmly believed that she might be able to contribute to bridging some gulfs and bringing people closer together—plus, of course, it was a way out of the cabaret circuit. As a result, she and her Tina band performed in Johannesburg, Durban, and Cape Town. Because there was no huge Sun City at the time, she was fortunate to avoid that sin and has since rejected any offers from it, despite receiving significant (and probably understandable) public criticism back then.

She was working her way back from the depths of cabaret exile after that problematic but financially necessary decision, and she needed all the aid she could get, so they worked out favorable tours of Australia and Southeast Asia. Somewhere along the road, the ever-observant Roger Davies discovered she was in desperate need of a style makeover. This Tina was neither the young soul-shaking Tina from the Revue nor the exquisite fierce dame Tina from after her resurrection was complete. Davies needed to change the lounge-age image and cabaret disco style, as well as remove the Las Vegas sparkle that he perceived as Bob Mackie-soaked Cher-ness (no insult to Cher fans, she's wonderful at what she does).

So they removed her outfit, her band, her dancers, her stage design crew, everything, and essentially started over. It was 1980, and everything was changing. MTV was due to begin in August of the following year, and they already had an insatiable demand for fresh mini-movies to sell songs and albums. Davies had an early instinctive understanding of the significance of videos, and he also knew that record executives were frequently mired in the past, so he sought a means to give birth to a new Tina Turner who would completely erase all memory (nearly but not quite) of the previous one. Music videos were the ideal medium for him to introduce his new Tina.

Her comeback was nearly live on television 24 hours a day. And she owed a lot to Roger Davies for its deft application. It was a medium tailor-made for Tina's showy character, and she, along with performers such as Michael Jackson and Madonna, would both capitalize on and reinvent the technology as an artistic form of expression. Her dazzling videos, which she produced in droves, were National Geographic documentaries of the passion she wore on her sleeve or, rather, on her skirt.

Tina Turner's first short films were released just in time to catch this new wave while it was in full swing and to define its parameters with her personal sense of style. Tina Turner's concerts were often described as "small movies," and she often described her concerts as "small movies." Even more than in her ostensibly straight acting parts in big-budget films, we see concrete and tactile evidence of her irresistible appeal in her music videos.

Furthermore, after an artist has passed away, and independent of their fans' experiences of seeing them live or hearing their albums, their films are frequently the sole historical document that can be consulted in order to study their theater skill. And hers were some of the most visually appealing in the new media.

Manager on a mission: the other, almost military-style tactic Davies used to promote his most daring client was more traditional but nonetheless effective: selectively placing her in select live gigs. He brought her to the Ritz in New York City, a city she hadn't visited in at least ten years, and he made certain that every superstar on the globe, those with long-term memories, packed the club to the rafters. Davies then orchestrated a People magazine cover story titled "The Return of Tina Turner," and then, realizing that her old guardian angels, the Rolling Stones, now the undisputed royalty of rock, were about to embark on yet another U.S. tour culminating with a slew of dates in New York, he choreographed a second stint at the Ritz.

Club owner Jerry Brandt agreed to bring her back, and her appearance drew her into the circle of rock icon Rod Stewart, who began nearly competing with fellow Brit rockers the Stones to see who could command the most of Tina's attention. The Stones had her all to themselves as the incendiary opening act for their tour, and she was the first to go.

Following her tour with the Stones, Stewart was performing live in Inglewood at the Great Western Forum for a concert that would be broadcast via satellite around the world, and he invited both Kim Carnes and Tina to duet with him on his song "Stay with Me," which he included on the Absolutely Live album he released. Tina knew what she wanted to do by this point: she wanted to be like the Rolling Stones, Rod Stewart, and all the other big-guy bands who were filling the large sports stadiums.

Rocker Rod had also appeared at her Ritz gig, accompanied by record producer Richard Perry, and stated that he was set to appear on Saturday Night Live and play his song "Hot Legs." Would the dame with the hottest legs in music be interested in joining him for a duet? Really? She had an unexpected audience of unfathomable millions, thanks to a Brit rock star who had worshiped her for years.

Meanwhile, Tina's old karmic pals the Stones were performing at the Forum at the time, and they were delighted when Tina's aggressive and inventive new manager Davies took her backstage for a catch-up. They admired her work with Rod on Saturday Night Live and were puzzled as to why she wasn't touring with them again. The band immediately booked her to open for them on their next stop, at the Brendan Byrne Arena, close to New York, a cozy little stadium offering 20,000 seats as well as a massive venue attracting every music honcho and critic in the industry.

On top of that incredible coup, Mick Jagger, ever the shrewd showman, asked Tina to join him onstage for a song duet of (what else?) "Honky Tonk Women." Needless to say, when the new Tina came loping onstage to meet Mick, with shorter, spiky, wigless hair in her form-hugging black leather pants and saucy leopard-skin boots, virtual pandemonium erupted. People immediately recognized — or remembered — how much she meant to them.

They also knew what they meant to her: vindication, validation, emancipation, not so much a comeback as the collective expression of a similar feeling: that she was a force of nature beyond anyone's control, possibly even her own. But it's also worth considering how ironically the label "tumultuous" applies to her.

Aaron Cohen reminded me that, while she appeared to be out of control on stage, she was a polished professional who was in complete control of her game at all times. "While she came across as unbridled onstage, I believe she also exhibited a great deal of control in terms of co directing/leading her bands (as part of the Ike and Tina Revue, or later on her own)." Similarly, her 1980s success in film and other areas of show business would not have been as effective if she didn't have a completely firm sense of self-control.``

John Corcelli had firsthand experience with what seemed to make that time, the early 1980s, just feel so suitable for Tina's rebirth as a solo pop artist after seeing her perform in Toronto in 1982, following her first two solo records and just prior to her grandiose third re-launch. "Her voice, as well as her sexuality." This was a woman who was completely at ease in her own skin and wasn't afraid to express it. On a more personal level, our musical heroes frequently represent who we desire to be. But, since we are terrified of failure, we live vicariously through them.

"Turner has a strong moral compass and a tenacious personality." You either like it or don't. Her character strength is what sets her apart from the rest of the pack." That appears to be an accurate appraisal of how we, as listeners, appeared ready to choose this particular fabled feminine figure as an emblem of our own ambitions and desires at that specific period in musical history.

The time had come for some new positive karma, and it arrived in the form of yet another appearance at the Ritz in New York, this time with a unique added attraction. Because David Bowie was in New York for a listening session for his latest album, Let's Dance, he was asked what he was doing after the session by a slew of record executives, promoters, critics, and general movers and shakers. He replied that he was going to see Tina Turner, his favorite artist. He once joked that anytime Tina Turner was on stage, that was the hottest spot in the globe.

So, guess who enthusiastically accompanied Bowie on his late-night outing to chill with him? Only half of the world's most prominent music industry figures. Naturally, they all wanted to be near the hottest spot in the cosmos. Backstage crushes included David Bowie and Keith Richards, who both wanted to escape to Keith's Park Plaza residence to listen to old music and drink champagne with Tina in tow after her outstanding performance, which was especially sexier than normal. They went around with Ron Wood and others, listening to old music, singing, drinking, dancing, and laughing until the next morning.

Following her spectacular Ritz performance, Capitol Records became interested in signing her up for new records, but the cunning and inventive Davies also wanted to approach EMI in England, where she still had an established foundation, so he arranged time at

Abbey Road studios to test out some stuff. They concentrated on an old Al Green song, "Let's Stay Together," from 1971, one of her peak years.

She knocked this song out of the park and utterly stole it from Al Green; as usual, she now owned that tune. Davies released it as a single and planned a large tour to correspond with a song that had become a smash hit in Europe despite Capitol Records' refusal to support it. They demonstrated a lack of vision, which was not surprising coming from a label brand that had frequently wrecked brilliant works by titans such as the Beatles and the Beach Boys due to a startling lack of creative sensitivity on their side.

Davies was on the move quickly, as was his main client (he was also managing Olivia Newton-John at the same time). He arranged a show at the Venue, a small club owned by Virgin Records, where she had to extend her run by more than a week to accommodate the frenetic audience demand. She then performed on Top of the Pops, and Davies recruited the show's producer to film a video of her singing "Let's Stay Together," along with her dancers Ann Behringer and Lejeune Richardson. It would be the first of many music videos she would create.

By the end of 1983, "Let's Stay Together" was a Top 5 smash in England and rapidly moving across the rest of Europe. Capitol Records finally succumbed and hurried the single's release forward after certain influential deejays aired the song on various famous black music radio stations. Capitol, ever the vultures in suits, immediately wanted to follow it up with an album to sustain the tsunami it had started. Davies, on the other hand, refused to return to America after committing to a large tour across Britain, a country for which Tina felt a tremendous feeling of devotion and appreciation. He persuaded Capitol to let them record their long-awaited album in an English studio instead.

While Tina took her band on tour, Davies remained in London to try to locate suitable material for an as-yet-unreleased record. He already had one song in mind, one that he and Tina both liked, written by Holly Knight for a band called Spider. It was named "Better Be

Good to Me." He and Tina wanted more songs for the album, so he contacted an old Australian buddy, Terry Britten, who had cowritten a song with Graham Lyle called "What's Love Got to Do with It?"" Davies wasn't convinced on this one. He scheduled studio time to capture it and continued his hunt for additional songs to compliment it because it was highly pop focused, albeit well-crafted pop.

Tina's initial reactions to "What Is Love?" were predictable."—not her style, even calling it "wimpy," but the writers and producers were ready to let her tinker with it and adjust the key or tempo to her liking. At the same time, she happened onto an unfinished song composed by Mark Knopfler of the band Dire Straits, simply a short track without a vocal put on it yet that had been left off their next album, Love over Gold. It was judged to be too "girly" for them.

Knopfler was a kind and approachable man, not your typical rock star, and he offered to perform a vocal merely to give them a sense of the tune, but he also gave them permission to re-record the track with Tina's pipes on it any way they wanted. Meanwhile, Capitol was keeping an eye on things from afar and sent producer John Carter over to keep things moving. The band was lacking its lead guitarist at the time, but an able-fingered guitarist who was ready to perform sessions on the song happened to be available: none other than iconic rock hero Jeff Beck.

They added "I Can't Stand the Rain" by Ann Peebles from 1973, as well as "Let's Stay Together," a racy romp by Paul Brady, and Bowie's "1984" to what they'd already been able to cram together through some bizarre alchemy. Rupert Hine, the Fixx's producer, has committed to produce the upcoming album. Davies was as happy as he could be despite having completely fried his nerves.

Capitol hastily released "What's Love Got to Do with It" to pique the public's interest in the soon-to-be-issued album. It quickly rose to the Top 50 on the pop charts. Tina had evolved far beyond her early rhythm-and-blues beginnings, as well as far beyond her rock-and-roll spirit and light-years away from her rock attitude, and had arrived in a bright and shiny place. This is what pop can be when everything is in order, like a well-oiled machine. The album now had a title, one that capitalized on that throwaway little unfinished tune that Knopfler had so kindly let them have, as well as many producers and a glittering technical quality associated with that decade. It was a song called "Private Dancer."

If the first half of her career was all about the Big Wheel Rolling, both together and apart, the second half would be about her incredible skill at Reinventing the Wheel, as her comeback continued frantically, with no sign of slowing down anytime soon. It still hasn't happened. Tina Turner's solo career saw her release nine astonishingly successful record albums (well, five fantastic ones), each one approaching and then surpassing the admittedly high-water marks she had set in her previous relationship.

She released two soundtrack albums, six compilation albums, three live concert albums, eighteen video albums, and forty-seven music videos, a medium that didn't even exist while she was working with her previous bandleader. In addition, following her release, she issued sixty singles, only eight shy of the total she had given throughout their sixteen-year cooperation.

The process by which this transformation occurred remains a mystery. Of course, times change, and she was wise enough to change with them. Even if she tapped into some cosmic vibration through her chanting practice as a means of both surviving her abuse and balancing her subsequent solitude, that can't explain her unexpected return and phoenix-like rise again, or her morphing with such apparent smoothness into a mega pop star of such grandiose proportions.

Discuss your transformations! Tina Turner was about to mutate yet again, this time into a scintillating pop star of epic proportions, after already evolving from a scrappy young rhythm-and-blues singer with a penchant for a spectral and soulful blues holler into a state-of-the-art rocker chick with Stones-scale arena credentials. And it only took half a decade of being off the grid to shed her skin in the most dramatic midlife crisis ever documented.

So, what do you do when you have two years to reflect after leaving your abusive husband and after two albums that were not met with wide arms by your legion of former fans? Perhaps you should start thinking about it. Apart from cleansing her personal slate emotionally before her comeback, the main motive for all her efforts seemed to be finding a method to convince people to stop asking her questions about her unhappy marriage and musical relationship.

She must have been earnestly contemplating how she could ever put an end to her insatiable interest regarding her upbringing and early creative career. How to stop the never-ending commemoration of what she believed would go away (in what decade, she had famously pondered). She secretly hoped, perhaps too innocently, that she would be permitted to go about her life and compose new music.
Yet, she must have instantly recognized, the key is embedded in that quandary. Yes, she deduced, made new music, but not just new music: music that is significantly different from anything and everything we've ever heard from her before. It's neither rhythm and blues, nor soul or funk, nor rock and roll or even rock; it's bluesy, but not in the classic sense.

It has a vaguely postmodern torch ballad feel to it, but only if you adhere to the technique beautifully articulated in that punchy Bowie song "Putting Out Fire with Gasoline." In the end, it can truly be defined as Tina goes pop!

(CAPITOL RECORDS) PRIVATE DANCER

The film was released on May 29, 1984. Farmyard Studios, Mayfair, Wessex, Abbey Road, and CBS (London) are among the locations. Rupert Hine, Terry Britten, John Carter, Martin Ware, Greg Walsh, Joe Sample, Wilton Felder, and Ndugu Chancler produced. The time is 44:02.

I Could Have Been Queen (Jeanette Obstoi, Jamie West-Oram) 4:10 / What Does Love Have to Do With It? (Terry Britten, Graham Lyle) 3:49 / Show Some Respect (Terry Britten, Sue Shifrin) 3:18 / I Can't Stand the Rain (Ann Peebles, Don Bryant, Bernard Miller) 3:41 / Better Be Good to Me (Mike Chapman, Holly Knight) 5:10 /

Some things in life are well worth the wait. This was one of them for a forty-five-year-old artist who had been in the profession for over thirty years. The charmer was her fifth solo studio album. Recording sessions took place in one of her favorite places, England, with four distinct production teams of eight people and material in almost as many different styles. It's safe to say it's a drastic change from all she'd become known for with the Revue, as well as everything that came after Ike.

Uptempo melodies coupled with sorrowful ballads and a difficult-to-describe jazzy blues aspect, all skillfully placed over her distinctive vocal talents, made it not just a smash solo record but also one of music history's most successful crossover products: a masterpiece of reinvention. It was rewarded with global popularity, multiple platinum certifications, and a commercial bonanza for Turner in her new persona, a spiky-haired vixen who posed somewhere between Aunty Entity and the Acid Queen, but also well beyond both.

It brilliantly captured the luxurious essence of the mid-1980s and provided her with a long-term legacy: the development of a historic event in the growth of not just pop rock but also pop pop. It was slick in its production values to the extreme but in a good way. It was flawless pop, period. She would fiercely promote it with a stunning stage show on a 177-date concert tour across the world: the Private Dancer Tour. Several tracks on this album are such appropriate manifestations of her ethos that they will be firmly carved in our memories, not only of her record but also of her difficult private life leading up to it.

"Better Be Good to Me," "Show Some Respect," "What's Love Got to Do With It," and, of course, the title track (which was strangely created for Mark Knopfler's Dire Straits band but kept back by fate for Tina) all became major single singles. The album is still the only Tina Turner record that has been digitally restored.

Of course, compliments poured in like rain. According to the Los Angeles Times, her voice "melts vinyl." Rolling Stone called it a consummate and powerful comeback, "rasping but strong, in a modern rock format neither detached nor fussy." Robert Christgau praised its ability to "deliver with honesty the middlebrow angst of professional songwriting, while remaining in control of an album with four different production teams to give it all seamless authority."

In the New York Times, Stephen Holden wrote that by using English producers to soften her raw southern style, "discarding the blaring horns, frenzied percussion, and gospel calls and responses, the album became a classic in the development of pop-soul music." Michael Lydon wrote in 1001 Albums You Must Hear Before You Die that the album's lyrical themes "embodied her persona as a tough, sexy woman in a tough world, one

Slant Magazine named the album one of the best albums of the 1980s, stating that "both a personal liberation and sonic redemption, Private Dancer established Turner not only as a genuine diva, but a bone fide force of nature." I second that sentiment, except for the diva part: she was always too down to earth to be described by that overused term. Surprisingly, it was also the album's various producers and diverse songwriting styles with varying emotional temps that made it a flawless pop record. Perfection in pop means it offered something for everyone, of every taste, age, and style demographic, which also means it sold well and Tina was back, big time.

Although the planning, production, and release were all rushed, and she wasn't quite convinced about the new high-tech pop musical content, she had learnt by then to trust Roger Davies and his maybe younger musical sensibilities. She was a savvy enough performer to realize that, even if she could argue that these weren't her type of music, they had no choice but to release the album. So she simply consented to whatever formula would result in a hit record. And it's apparent that her adaptability paid off.

One thing she enjoyed about the album, once she got used to the synths and computerized production, was how hard it rocked while also avoiding certain rhythm-and-blues cliches that had always irritated her, things like its whining and pleading attitude that were a turnoff for her. She had come to really appreciate the straight-ahead energy of rock and roll and how you wanna put it on to get you going for quite some time before this occasion.

Keith Richards, a rock specialist and possibly her biggest fan, agreed with both her tastes and intentions on this record, telling *Newsweek*, "She's probably even more energetic than she was twenty years ago!""—and that's saying a lot. Without a doubt, it was a combination of her newly gained independence, working solely for herself rather than for a music maestro, and a determination to have as much fun as possible in life in general from now on.

She is quoted in *Off the Record* as claiming that she felt more confident than ever about performing. "I'm a strong, healthy person because I'm homeopathic and never abuse my body." I'm an uncommon person; I could perform a show right now. I would not have come as far as I did if I had abused myself (with drugs or alcohol) in the beginning. "I'm healthy and in command."

Tina, never one to loiter about patiently waiting for much of anything, went on a four-month tour opening for Lionel Ritchie while *Private Dancer* was undergoing its complex surgical production procedure. Much of the album harkened back to her own personal, professional, and private life, despite the fact that none of the songs were specifically about her, instead being a cleverly sculpted techno-dance record of distinctly different parts that just happened to capture the zeitgeist feeling of the time. The literal translation of the German word Zeitgeist, which sounds eerily close to Poltergeist (which means "noise ghost"), is "time ghost."

And Tina Turner had proven herself to be in some exotic way—not necessarily timeless (though she is some of that as well), but more in the sense of being displaced from one time and emerging into another, a person out of time entirely and definitely a person ahead of her time in many ways.

Listeners and critics alike fell in love with both the record *Private Dancer* and the new Tina Turner behind it. She performed in every conceivable venue and for every conceivable show, all over radio and television, spinning endlessly on MTV and being extolled by magazines as the grittiest rock-and-roll singer in the world despite the fact that she was no longer exactly a rocker and instead was "something else." My contention is that she had already been a rock star for years, but this venture transformed her into a bona fide pop star, which by my definition is music so universally appealing

Private Dancer reached number three on the pop charts in September 1984 and remained there for three months. The album naturally prompted former Capital to issue further singles from it, including "Better Be Good to Me," "Private Dancer," and a Euro smash, "I Can't Stand the Rain." The album lingered in the Top 100 for more than two years and eventually sold 19 million copies.

She finished 1984 by traveling in a range of American and Canadian performance dates that had previously been planned before the release of her new album, which went full ballistic throughout its ascension. Returning to America for the American Music Awards on January 28, 1985, she won several top prizes in female vocals and video performer slots before joining a small group of forty-two of her fellow musical super-stars for a ten-hour recording session aimed at raising funds for African famine relief. It was a moving humanist anthem called "We Are the World."

I asked James Porter, a black rock historian, how he would address Tina's later music's change from harder to gentler musical moods. "I think her solo records are 'lighter,' but only in the sense that they aren't as bluesy as they were when Ike was around." The influence was still there—she covered a couple of Tony Joe White songs—but it wasn't as strong. However, I believe that the later records are equally as serious musically as the early sides. ..However, in a different direction. Listening to songs like 'Private Dancer' now may sound like an ironic dry run for an INXS album, but Tina's Voice of Experience steps in and sets the record right." Indeed, setting the record straight was always what she was about, from start to finish.

Tina Turner captivated the entire Grammy Awards event in February 1985 with a performance of "What's Love Got to Do with It?"," and she received Grammy nominations for best female pop vocal, best female rock vocal, and record of the year for "What's Love Got to Do With It?""When she soaked up the roaring affection of the crowd, possibly expressing their spirited respect for her dogged survival nearly as much as her tremendous musical triumph, she intoned in that unmistakable breathy rasp of hers, "We're looking forward to many more of them."

Around the same time, her now-extremely foresighted manager Roger Davies told Vogue that one of the things that disturbed her the most was that people and the press continued to refer to her as a victim in her previous life. "She was so unhappy for so long, she can't stand it when it gets too dark, and she hates it when people feel sorry for her," she said succinctly to GQ magazine. "The victim thing, it's put in our heads, and I don't think it does anybody any good really."

Perhaps unsurprisingly, Hollywood was calling once more. She'd often remarked, usually just fantasizing aloud, that she'd love to obtain another larger-than-life movie role, something even more outrageous than Tommy's Acid Queen part, something along the lines (she hoped) of Grace Jones' role in Conan the Destroyer. As icing on the cake, Roger Davies had come to her hotel when she was playing the Ritz and told her he'd just received a call from director George Miller offering her a major role in his forthcoming Mad Max picture. Suddenly, her life appeared to be a genuine dream rather than the toxic nightmare it had previously been.

Tina would play Auntie Entity, a bizarre Amazon figure who is the matriarchal warlord of an outlying city named Bartertown in Beyond Thunderdome. She was thrilled to be playing another Queen for the second time in ten years. Not only that, but she'd be singing two songs in the film: the iconic "We Don't Need Another Hero," a curious counterpart to one of her favorite Bowie lyrics about being heroes "just for one day," and "One of the Living," which ended up in a massively visible position playing over the Maurice Jarre film titles. Naturally, this entailed the release of a soundtrack album.

BEYOND THE THUNDERDOME (MAD MAX) (CAPITOL RECORDS)

It was released in 1985. Terry Britten and Graham Lyle (who also created her hit "What's Love Got to Do With It") produced the movie soundtrack recording. Tina Turner on vocals, Charlie Moran on drums, Kings School Choir, Nick Glennie-Smith on keyboards, Graham Bond on percussion, Tim Cappello on saxophone, Terry Britten on guitar, Holly Knight on keyboards, Gene Black on backup vocals, and Charles McMahon on didgeridoo. The video lasts 44:27 minutes.

6:05 / One of the Living (Holly Knight) 5:59 / Hero Instrumental (Terry Britten, Graham Lyle) 6:30 / Bartertown (Maurice Jarre) 8:28 / The Children (Maurice Jarre) 2:11 / Coming Home (Maurice Jarre) The film's blockbuster soundtrack music, produced by Maurice Jarre and played by the Royal Philharmonic Orchestra, also included twenty-six minutes of orchestral score performed by the Royal Philharmonic Orchestra. Turner's U.S. number two and U.K. number one positions, however, stood out for fans. "We Don't Need Another Hero," the movie's number three single, played over the end credits. The single was released a year after Turner's album Private Dancer. In 1986, the song was nominated for a Golden Globe for best original song and a Grammy for best pop female vocal performance. The film's opening title piece, composed by Mike Chapman and Holly Knight, was the second Turner tune on the album; the song won Turner a Grammy Award in 1985 for best rock female vocal performance. This film sequel's soundtrack was a far cry from the first and grittier Brian May (Queen) approach, but Jarre managed to pull it off with remarkable elegance in his own language.

Mad Max Beyond Thunderdome, as AllMusic critic James Monger noted at the time, divided critics and fans alike with its big-budget rendition of Gibson's legendary vigilante. "What sounded strange in theory came across much better on film." Jarre put up an immaculate storm of a soundtrack that paid homage to May's brutal dissonance while generating a distinctive melody—The Children—and bringing a harmonic lushness that was lacking in the early films."

Her outrageous Aunty Entity role is actually ideal for her. The character, like the singer, is a powerful lady. Turner has never wanted to make a sensual film and claims she isn't funny, therefore she wanted to deal with some form of conflict, with physical power in a woman. It's her fundamental personality, the way she's built. When asked about potential film parts, she told Maclean's magazine, "I want to do really heroic women things." "I'd like to play a female version of Sylvester Stallone's Rambo."

Her personal karma had apparently kicked in and was propelling her forward at full throttle once more. It was as if she had not only become a female archetype signifying survival, but also triumph, and that portion of the collective unconscious we all share, consisting of tremendous metaphors, had emerged from wherever it sits. And then, as if on cue, Stephen Spielberg called to give her the lead role in his film adaptation of Alice Walker's narrative The Color Purple. But she opted, quite properly, I believe, to turn that one down, no matter how big a deal it would have been, perhaps realizing that the narrative was literally too close to home. "I know that story!"", she explained at the time.

Given her commitment to valor and strength, it was no surprise that Spielberg contacted her to be the major female actress in his Purple remake, and it was also no surprise that she gently declined the generous offer. Personally, she believed that black people could do better, and she declined because it was too close to her personal life, and it was far too recent to be reminded of it. Although she was thrilled and delighted to be asked to be in Spielberg's film, it was simply the wrong role for her at the time.

Keeping connected to her personal musical interests was probably also a wise professional decision. Apart from her main job description of playing Tina Turner, acting had always been a bit of a sideline for her. In 1985, she joined a large cross-section of worldwide stars for a global rock-and-roll Live Aid telecast, and the mid-1980s singles continued to roll. Her single "We Don't Need Another Hero" peaked at number three in the United Kingdom, and her video for "What's Love Got to Do with It?" won best female video at the second annual MTV Video Awards ceremony; that fall, the single for "One of the Living" (her second Mad Max song) peaked at number 15 in America; and at the end of the year, she received an NAACP Image Award for best actress for her role in Mad Max Beyond Thunderdome.

The 1980s were a great time in her already incredible life, especially being able to play in front of large mixed-race audiences. Clubs and theaters had been left in the dust, and she had evolved into a massive arena show on par with Queen and Elton John. It's what made the concept of Break Every Rule so ideal for a new album theme. "When we're talking about those guys who can pack those football stadiums, we're talking about the men that all the girls love," she told Vogue. So it's like violating the rules for me to be with them." Tina clearly enjoys bending and then shattering every assumption that comes her way.

EVERY RULE IS BROKEN (CAPITOL RECORDS)

It was released in 1986. Terry Britten, Bryan Adams, Bob Clearmountain, Rupert Hine, Mark Knopfler, and Neil Dorfsman produced the album. Bryan Adams on guitar; Terry Britten on bass and vocals; Samantha Brown on vocals; Jack Bruno on drums; Tim Cappello on saxophone; Margo Buchanan on vocals; Richard Elen on sound design; Mickey Feat on bass; Nick Glennie-Smith on keyboards; Gary Katell on percussion; Steve Winwood on synthesizer; Tina Turner on lead vocals. The time is 50:13.
4:18 / What You Get Is What You See (Terry Britten, Graham Lyle) 4:31 / Two People (Terry Britten, Graham Lyle) 4:11 / Till the Right Man Comes Along (Terry Britten, Graham Lyle) 4:11 / Afterglow (Terry Britten, Graham Lyle) 4:30 / Girls (David Bowie, Erdal Kizilcay) 4:56

The original vinyl version's A-side was produced by the award-winning team behind "What's Love Got to Do With It?"," Terry Britten and Graham Lyle, with Bryan Adams, Rupert Hine, and Mark Knopfler producing the B-side. Tina also recorded a duet with Eric Clapton after this session, which was included on Phil Collins' 1986 album August. Break Every Rule was an international hit, peaking at number four on the Billboard 200 and number two in the United Kingdom. Number one on the Albums Chart, as well as in Germany and Switzerland.

The album went on to sell 12 million copies, was certified platinum, and is still well-known today. Tina went on a big world tour to promote it, including a filmed concert date in Rio de Janeiro, Brazil, where she performed in front of over 180,000 people, as well as several additional concerts that would be taped for release two years later.

Her Break Every Rule album followed the same formula as Private Dancer, with a few key exceptions: no cover songs, entirely new material, a tighter focus, and a lineup of other megawatt stars to make it rock out the way she loved it. Brian Johnson witnessed the first show of her 1985 cross-country tour in Canada and wrote in Maclean's magazine about how she "shimmied, strutted, and slithered her way into the hearts and libidos of about 5,000 fans packed into a hockey arena." Tina Turner has never been hotter at the age of 46."

Her new single "Show Some Respect" debuted at number 37 on the charts in June of that year, the same month her wild turn as an action heroine debuted in Mad Max Beyond Thunderdome. It's fair to say she was gaining well-deserved acclaim, and music fans appeared to be in desperate need of another international heroine.

1986 will also be remembered as the year she finally broke her public silence regarding her difficult early years with Ike. Tina was once again baring her soul to the press, which she appeared to enjoy doing. She was more comfortable ruminating in her customary intimate fashion about where she was in her life, how she got there, and where she was heading following the tidal wave of her first great comeback smash, and literally only weeks after the release of her racy follow-up to it, Break Every Rule.

She was even fine with Rolling Stone magazine naming her the Queen of Rock and Roll, even though by 1986, she had clearly established herself as the Queen of Pop. She had consolidated her actual achievements as a woman of the 1980s, not only as a recipient of huge wealth, but also for the joys of emancipation after surviving in a business notorious for exploitation of women. She became an emblem of sorts, a living embodiment of simple survival instincts, in addition to the devotion of many fans (and possibly almost as significant to her).

She attributes her durability to Roger Davies, the new manager who oversaw her return to the top of the rock-and-roll world with the shimmering pop masterpieces Private Dancer and Break Every Rule. The title of Turner's second album is also relevant, since she is plainly at a crossroads in her life when she hardly acknowledges the existence of rules, let alone submits to them.

And, in some ways, the concept that, as her new record suggested, she breaks every norm is possibly unwittingly linked to a self-deprecating attitude she still possessed. The remarkable thing is that someone who had accomplished so much, both emotionally and professionally, could still feel a deep absence in some way that was clearly linked to her background.

Her closest friends knew she was still looking for the respect she believed she earned, as well as the recognition of a sense of classiness she had always desired. At this point in her life, at the age of forty-six, she was still yearning for the affection of the type of man she believed she deserved. Not only was it coming, but Erwin Bach had already discreetly entered her life through the back door—that very year.

Tina won for best female rock vocal performance for her song "Back Where You Started" in 1987, but she was definitely a long way from where she started. She had become her own personal, real-life Rocket 88! "I'm not looking for pity about my life with Ike," she told Life at the time. "It was many years ago. "I'm done with it," she said in 1993, the year the film adaptation was released, to GQ magazine on the difficulty of reliving the past. "I drank a lot of wine, but I got through it." "The entire world was stunned." We are still stunned.

Tina Turner's 1988 was simply another new solo album release, one commemorating her massive concert tours in favor of both Private Dancer and Break Every Rule. And a live Tina record was as least as interesting as a live Ike and Tina album, if not more so.

TINA RESIDES IN EUROPE. (CAPITOL RECORDS/EMI)

It was released in 1988. Terry Britten and John Hudson produced. Personnel: Tina Turner, vocals; Jamie Ralston, guitar; Bob Feit, bass and vocals; Jack Bruno, drums; Stevie Scales, percussion; John Miles, keyboards; Ollie Marland, keyboards and vocals; Deric Dyer, saxophone and keyboards; Jamie West-Oram, guitar; Don Snow, keyboards; Tim Cappello, keyboards and saxophone; Alan Clark, keyboards; Kenny Moore, keyboards; Gary Barnacle, saxophone. Birmingham, Wembley, London, and Camden, England; Westfallenhalle, Dortmund, West Germany; and Issadion, Stockholm, Sweden are the venues. The time is 121:54.

The First Disc: What You See Is What You Get (Terry Britten, Graham Lyle) Break Every Rule (Rupert Hine, Jeannette Obstoi) 5:34 I Can't Stand the Rain (Ann Peebles) 4:28 Three and a Half Minutes (Terry Britten, Graham Lyle) Typical Male (Terry Britten, Graham Lyle) 4:26 Better Be Good to Me (3:59) (Holly Knight, Nicky Chinn, Mike Chapman) Addicted to Love (Robert Palmer) 6:29 5:22 / Mark Knopfler's Private Dancer We Don't Need Another Hero (Terry Britten, Graham Lyle) (5:37) What Does Love Have to Do With It? (Terry Britten, Graham Lyle) 4:56 Let's Stay Together (Al Green, Willie Mitchell, and Al Jackson) 5:28 Show Some Respect (Terry Britten, Sue Shirin) 4:40 Disc 2: Land of a Thousand Dances (Chris Kenner) 3:05 In the Midnight Hour (Wilson Pickett, Steve Cropper) 3:06 (Eddie Floyd, Steve Cropper) 3:32 / 634-5789 3:05 / Sam Cooke's A Change Is Gonna Come River Deep, Mountain High (Phil Spector, Ellie Greenwich, and Jeff Barry) 6:44 Tearing Us Apart (Eric Clapton, Greg Phillinganes) 4:11 4:41 / John Fogerty's "Proud Mary" Help! (John Lennon, Paul McCartney) 4:47 Tonight (David Bowie, Iggy Pop) 5:03 Let's Dance (David Bowie) 4:15 Overnight Sensation (Mark Knopfler) 3:27 It's Only Love (Bryan Adams) 3:54 4:15 / Tina Turner's Nutbush City Limits 3:43 / Paul Brady's Paradise Is Here 5:41

This is Tina Turner's debut live solo album, a collection of concert performances from 1985 to 1987, including dates from her Break Every Rule Tour as well as her Private Dancer Tour, as well as live material from her HBO special in London. In 1989, this concert recording was nominated for a Grammy Award for best female rock performance. The record, which passionately documented several of her most successful performances during her winning tour, reached number 8 in England, and it's an ideal audio archive indeed.

Some of us were lucky enough to witness her play live in concert, while others were not. For those of us who missed her, here was an album that captured some of the fervor in her personal delivery and made us feel like we were part of the vast European audience writhing in delight as she gave the gift of her classics, both old and new.

When she performed live, she was always incredibly generous with her audience, well knowing that they had paid top cash to see her, and when they left the stadia or theaters, she had just one goal in mind: she wanted them to feel as blissed out as humanly possible. She typically succeeded in that goal, as listeners of this double record set may confirm.

But her enormous success—and her personal involvement with both struggle and triumph—is nonetheless tempered by the now-long standing spiritual equanimity that so many people associate with her basic, daily, down-to-earth personality: big but humble.

CHAPTER 7:
RE-LAUNCH

Tina Turner has credited her early encounter with Buddhism for the dramatic reversal in her life, altering her old established habits of thought about who she was, what she was, and what she was capable of doing, all along the way and to this day. Who can deny the validity of her argument? Because her outer reality began to reflect that positive inner attitude almost like a mirror, to the point where she feels a calling to engage in teaching some of what she's discovered about the spiritual life when she's finished with the entertainment industry.

Until then, however, and thank whatever gods exist for this, she's still actively with us in the sweaty carnal world, or what George Harrison referred to as "living in the material world," because we need strong warrior women like her to keep us company in the midst of chaos. "My career is still in bloom," she said in her testimonial, and I've always found it moving. I'm not ready to teach anyone. When I'm ready, I'll devote all of my time to this and share what I've learnt. Many of you will listen, while others will hear."

You don't need to know anything about Buddhism to understand what she's saying, and you don't need to understand the enticing spiritual concept of deeds and their consequences to enjoy what she's delivering. Miss Bullock was a true living example of both terrible and good karma coming to fruition, of eventually receiving precisely what she deserved. Everyone, it seems, eventually sits down to a meal of consequences.

In some ways, the only other component of her life that could be hoped for, wanted for, and dreamed of was a deep romance and personal relationship with a nice and kind partner, someone who recognized who she truly was. But that was also on the way. Her good karma had not yet finished with her. Not by any means.

Perhaps the title of her impending 1989 album, Foreign Affair, referred to something more mundane, such as a foreign affair? For three years, she had been singing her now-signature song about what love had to do with it. How many times does someone have to think who needs a heart since our hearts might be broken before they look up and find a reason not just to have one but also to share it with another person? Of course, given her little experience with personal relationships, it had to be a challenge, but if anyone deserved to meet someone worth sharing her life with, it had to be Anna Mae Bullock. Foreign, if only in name, because it was in Europe that she received both her first recognition as a celebrity and her restored acceptance as a regenerated artist seeking a second chance. Europe had always welcomed her with open arms, and it turned out that a European guy, seventeen years her junior, would be the one to win her heart and, she would say, entirely embrace her soul. I don't want to abuse the term "karma," but what do you call it when you meet the man of your dreams by coincidence when he drops off a jeep for you to use while exploring Germany?

Call it fate, destiny, or serendipity if the word "karma" makes you uncomfortable. It scarcely matters, but that's the word Tina would naturally use in such a situation. She presents a compelling case for her acts and the repercussions of her actions leading her to meet someone extraordinary enough to deal with her history, energy, and future, someone remarkable enough to click in an instant, even if it would take three years for their relationship to actually take off.

Also, this would be someone concerned enough to accompany her through her upcoming health challenges, to be by her side during medical treatments for intestinal cancer, to donate one of his own kidneys in the event of a transplant, and even to cope with the trauma of his donated kidney being rejected and resulting in seizures and strokes. This is what some people call a mensch, a real person, and Erwin Bach, a German record executive, appears to be just such a man. They first met in 1985 during her Private Dancer Tour and decided they didn't actually need to marry, and only after a twenty-seven-year courtship did they do so in Switzerland in 2013.

She was suddenly as busy as she'd ever been in the 1960s by the 1980s, but it was a new kind of busy, a second blossoming, without the evident pressures associated with her initial wild ride into celebrity and misery. She's revealed that it appeared to be an immediate romance, the magical love-at-first-sight feeling we've all read about. Indeed, it was a heart-pounding moment, but her innate prudence in such issues forced her to wait three years before eventually committing to what her heart was screaming at her.

Following their chance meeting, she had been having a birthday party for a friend in West Hollywood at Wolfgang Puck's first Spago, and they had all retreated to her home in Sherman Oaks. Bach happened to be among them. Many witnesses saw that something remarkable began to happen during that party. She had purposefully leased a property in Switzerland and invited him to a Christmas party there with common friends in 1988, after their initial chance encounter and was interested in pursuing him further. The relationship just continued to flourish and evolve spontaneously from there, taking on a life of its own.

Her adult second career was blossoming, and her love life appeared to be doing the same. Against all odds, including being introduced to a family who may have been a little concerned about his new relationship with someone older than him (she was forty-eight at the time, he was thirty-one), being an American black rock star to boot, and despite the fact that they may have harbored some secret desires that the woman of his dreams might be a German (and a white one), they quickly fell in love with her as well. Everyone appears to eventually.

Her hectic career, on the other hand, was still flying high, and it needed to be addressed as well, especially in 1989. She performed in front of not only the largest crowd of fans she'd ever had as an audience, but also the largest crowd ever recorded anywhere. During her Break Every Rule Tour, she drew more than a quarter-million adoring fans at the Maracana Arena in Rio de Janeiro, prompting Guinness World Records to publish an official entry to that effect. When the trip came to an end in Osaka, Japan, she continued to break all house records.

Things continued to pick up speed. She attended the Grammy Awards shortly after visiting New York in January 1989 for the Rock and Roll Hall of Fame induction ceremony, where she inducted her old producer Phil Spector into the hallowed ranks of music legends, and won her seventh trophy in the category of best rock vocal performance for her Live in Europe album. Her next album, Foreign Affair, was released to critical acclaim and peaked at number one in the United Kingdom and number 31 in the United States. "The Best," the album's first hit, would go on to become one of her signature songs.

On November 26, 1989, she celebrated her fiftieth birthday with close rock mates such as Mark Knopfler, Eric Clapton, and Bryan Adams, and while it may seem like a long time, half a century was only getting started for her. Even for someone with legs like hers, saying she hit her stride in the next decade of the 1990s would be an understatement.

(EMI/CAPITOL RECORDS) FOREIGN AFFAIR

It was released in 1989. Dan Hartman, Tina Turner, Rupert Hine, Roger Davies, Graham Lyle, Albert Hammond, and Tony Joe White produced. Tony Joe White, guitar; Dan Hartman, acoustic guitar; Eddie Martinez, rhythm guitar; Neil Taylor, guitar; Mark Knopfler, guitar; Elliot Lewis and Nick Glennie-Smith, strings; Gary Barnacle, saxophones; Edgar Winter, saxophones; Phil Ashley, keyboards; Jeff Bova, synthesizers; Casey Young, keyboards; Carmine Roja and Rupert Hine, bass; J. Drums: T. Lewis and Art Wood; percussion: Albert Hammond; backing vocals: Lance Ellington, Sandy Stewart, and Tessa Niles; extra vocals: Roger Davies, Graham Lyle, and Holly Knight. Chris Lord-Alge, Andrew Scarth, Mike Ging, Nick Froome, and Tom Fritze worked on the sound design and mixing. Ezee, Mayfair, and Swanyard studios were used for overdubs. The video lasts 52:16 minutes.

5:20 / Look Me in the Heart (Tom Kelly, Billy Steinberg) 3:46 / Be Tender with Me Baby (Albert Hammond, Holly Knight) 4:18 / Can't Stop Me Loving You (Albert Hammond, Holly Knight) 4:00 / Ask Me How I Feel (Albert Hammond, Holly Knight) 4:46 / Falling Like Rain (David Munday, Sandy Stewart)

Tina was, of course, in the midst of a foreign romance, which would eventually lead to her second marriage. One recurring irony in Tina's career was that she was always having a foreign affair with music enthusiasts in Europe and the rest of the globe, one that always outlasted her American fans. It was simply a fascinating demographic to her tale.

This was her eighth solo studio album and the third release after her enormous return hit six years prior. It did not perform as well as Private Dancer or Break Every Rule, but it was still a massive hit in Europe and abroad. It peaked at number one in the United Kingdom. Albums Chart and sold over 6 million copies, as well as reaching number one in both Germany and Sweden and dominating the overall European charts for over a month.

Six of the album's twelve tunes became number one smash singles in Europe, with "Foreign Affair" and "The Best " becoming staples of her live performances ever since. By this point, she was a global pop phenomenon, and some younger listeners may not have been aware of her extensive previous background as a rhythm-and-blues torture or a rock queen.

With her latest hit "Steamy Windows" steaming up the charts, she embarked on a 121-date globe concert tour to promote Foreign Affair on April 27, ostensibly while still conducting said affair secretly. During the course of the performance tour, she entertained more than 3 million ecstatic fans, beginning in Antwerp, Belgium, and concluding in Rotterdam, Holland.

At the same time she was joyfully, even exultantly, delivering joy to half the world, her ex-husband was making vague headlines of his own, but for the opposite reasons. He'd been arrested eleven times in his fourteen years without Tina for a variety of offenses, and finally, in 1990, he was imprisoned for cocaine violations, drug transportation, and a few other assorted bad lifestyle difficulties.

Meanwhile, Tina's new album, Simply the Best, a greatest-hits collection, was released in October, featuring all of her most popular tunes from the 1980s, as well as a brand-new version of "Nutbush" and three new songs by her: "I Want You Near Me," "Way of the World," and "Love Thing."

EMI/CAPITOL RECORDS' SIMPLY THE BEST

It was released in 1991. Various producers, as stated in the originals. Her first greatest-hits collection, published on October 22, 1991, comprised her most popular songs produced between 1973 and 1991, with a focus on her songs since her huge comeback in 1984. The collection is her best-selling record in the United Kingdom, selling over 2.4 million copies, being certified 8x platinum, and being on their hit lists for more than 140 weeks in a row, with worldwide sales over 7 million.

The Australian special edition included five new bonus tracks, including a rerecording of "The Best" as a duet with Jimmy Barnes titled "Simply (The Best)," which was released as a single, as well as a new song, "I'm a Lady," which was released as a single and B-side to "Love Thing." Personnel is as recorded. (It's understandable that no tracks from her Rough or Love Explosion albums were selected.) The Best (Mike Chapman, Holly Knight) 4:10 / What's Love Got to Do With It (Terry Britten, Graham Lyle) 3:50 / I Can't Stand the Rain (Ann Peebles, Bryant Miller) 3:44 / I Don't Wanna Lose You (Albert Hammond, Graham Lyle) 4:18 / Nutbush City Limits (Tina Turner) 3:39 /

Simply the Best reached number two in the United Kingdom, and on her fifty-second birthday in 1991, she received a Quintuple Platinum Award for sales of 1.5 million copies of Foreign Affair. She rounded out the middle of 1992 by celebrating the end of her long-term Capitol Records contract in July and signing a fresh new deal with a brand-new firm, Virgin Records, which gave her creative life a new lease on life. Life was wonderful, and the future appeared to be getting brighter.

The past, on the other hand, is never truly dead; in fact, as William Faulkner once lamented, it isn't even past. And her ex-husband's lengthy shadow continued to disturb her activities—not so much derail them as sour them. Takin' Back My Name: The Confessions of

Ike Turner, authored with the assistance of Nigel Cawthorne and issued in 1999, was his own skewed "side" of the tale in which he grumbled publicly about his ex-wife's open reporting of events surrounding their life together.

By this point in her life, she always spoke haltingly (if at all) about her ex-husband in general, but she still managed to express considerable compassion for someone who treated her the way he did. Friends were well aware that her newfound peace of mind contained no desire for vengeance or resentment. It just wasn't her Buddhist way, so when he was eventually released from prison, she later demonstrated genuine happiness for him, perhaps conscious that he might even return to making his own music, which was always a primary cause of any happiness he ever experienced in his rough-and-tumble life.

Most readers, I believe, would agree with my assessment that Tina was expressing a deep feeling conveyed by a person of extraordinarily strong character—and compassion under the circumstances. Tina had already relocated permanently to Europe by the problematic time of his significantly skewed book's attempt at name rehabilitation (or rewriting history), and she no longer wished to memorialize that previous part of her life.

She left America primarily because her greatest success had always been in another country, and Europe had always been quite supportive of her music. Furthermore, her new boyfriend lived there, and she openly revealed that after living in England for a few years and then in her new partner's hometown of Cologne, Germany, they had settled nicely in Switzerland. Despite being born and raised in America, she felt as if she had never known her true home until she moved to Europe.

It's one thing to flee your life, or even your nation, but it's quite another to flee your history. The first two are doable if you're brave enough; the third is more obstinate and demands an even more iron will to endure. Tina Turner had turned a corner in terms of music, business, and love, but she still had to deal with the consequences of her own painful childhood experiences. She'd been popular before, but now that she was a major pop sensation, an even greater number of newer followers naturally wanted to know her personal history.

Her ex-husband's continued unlawful escapades prompted a slew of new news stories and interviews, as did her 1986 testimonial book, which blossomed into that massive Hollywood film in 1993. That film appears to have pushed Ike over the precipice he was already on. Fortunately for her, the induction of Ike and Tina Turner into the Rock and Roll Hall of Fame in 1991 occurred before his release from prison, so she avoided the embarrassing episode of either accepting a hugely important award with him nearby or failing to attend one of the most important events in her career.

She got lucky and was inducted alongside LaVern Baker, John Lee Hooker, the Impressions, Jimmy Reed, and the great Wilson Pickett, soaking up the adoration of a massive audience of both attendees and viewers from all over the world, some of whom had only known her since her triumphant return in 1984. Ike could only witness the official induction of his namesake Revue collaboration from the comfort of his jail cell at the time, during her Hall of Fame induction. However, after the film based on her life was released, everyone on the earth seemed to be aware of her traumatic young tragedy. It seemed like deja vu all over again.

Disney Corporation and Touchstone Films had purchased the rights to make I, Tina, based on her testimonial, and had also paid her ex-husband a significant enough money that he would agree to accept the representation without recourse to lawsuits if he was unsatisfied. They expected him to be upset considering how he was portrayed for public consumption.

He would subsequently say that he only signed the agreement because he was still high on drugs and didn't comprehend what he was doing.

In a GQ magazine feature at the time of its debut, she stated that the film was both real and narratively molded to fit the dramatic format, as is often the case when a story is adapted for the screen. "I've got to admit that they took the idea of my life and sort of wrote around it."

She felt that much was left out of the story, such as the very valid parts of the creative process of making music in the early days before things went off the rails, as well as her positive family life with her children.

But she accepted their decision to not only take certain liberties with facts, but also to focus on her meeting, performing, and recording with, marrying, enduring abuse from, and then escaping from her psychotic husband. Except for any "poetic liberties" done with chronology or events for the sake of dramatic reduction into two hours, all they portrayed was true. She only wished they had shown more of the occasional pleasant times and human interactions that made it all bearable—and maybe even survivable—at the end.

Some of the narrative differences she discovered were obvious to most people who had followed her life and music: Ike did not sing or play guitar on his early song "Rocket 88" as depicted, instead writing and playing piano; the song Anna Mae first performs onstage with Ike, "You Know I Love You" by BB King, was actually a much slower down-tempo blues ballad than depicted; the first song Anna Mae records, called "Tina's Wish" in

In the film, a theater marquee announcing a 1960 show starring Otis Redding, Martha and the Vandellas, and Ike and Tina Turner is shown, but in reality, Martha's group was known as the Del-Phis until 1961, and Otis did not become a solo act until 1962; in the film, Anna Mae learns of her name change to Tina Turner after a song featuring Ike and Tina Turner is played on the radio, but Tina had already Her first violent altercation with Ike came after she raised her concerns over the name change, and he hit her with a shoe stretcher.
The film suggests or implies that Tina's firstborn son, Craig, was Ike's biological child, but Craig was the son of Ike's saxophone player Raymond Hill, with whom Tina was briefly allied; the film depicts the couple marrying after Ike and his gang sneak Tina out of the hospital, but Ike was not present for the birth of their son, and Tina checked herself out of the hospital when she discovered that Ike had hired a prostitute to im

The film showed a reenactment clip of an interview the couple did in 1964 rather than 1971, when the real-life couple were in a similar context (Tina speaking throughout the interview with Ike remaining silent with his back to Tina and smoking a cigarette); in a scene dated 1968 in the film, the couple opened for the Rolling Stones, performing "Proud Mary," but in reality, they didn't perform that song until after Creedence Clearwater Revival released it

Most dangerously, the film depicts Tina's suicide attempt in 1974 (for unknown reasons) when it actually occurred in 1968; during the time Tina is planning her comeback in the early 1980s, a reenactment of an interview features her rehearsing her song "I Might Have Been Queen," but that song wasn't recorded until her album Private Dancer was produced; and in the film, before performing "What's Love Got to Do with It?" at the Ritz in New York, the emcee claims that it was her first performance, despite the fact that she had previously played there in 1981. Her appearance there in 1983 took place prior to the recording of her signature song and resulted in Capitol Records securing a recording contract with her.

Some aspects needed to be changed, and Tina was never proud of how the film presented her as a "victim" when her own perspective on her story was far more complex and nuanced. But, hey, this is Hollywood, and movies are like magic lanterns that sell both dreams and nightmares. The screenplay was adapted by Kate Lanier, and the film was directed by Brian Gibson and produced by Doug Chapin and Barry Krost, with the film generating around $40 million and $20 million in rentals, while it grossed £10 million alone in the United Kingdom, where she has a huge fan base.

Angela Bassett received a Golden Globe Award, Laurence Fishburne received an Oscar nomination, and the film garnered an American Choreography Award for several of its dance sequences. Fishburne was offered the job five times before accepting, allegedly concerned that it did not adequately address the fundamental causes of her ex-husband's behavior or why someone like Tina would stay with him for sixteen years. Many of Tina's most graphic claims of his assault, however, were not featured in the film. Tina was shocked that the film was made at all, according to the liner notes of the original film soundtrack on Virgin Records.

She never imagined her story would be made into a picture when the Disney Company purchased the film rights to it. It also astonished her how nicely some of the songs had held up over time. She recorded three new songs for the soundtrack and was on the road again in May, previewing a few of the new songs, when she went to Monaco and was honored with a trophy for outstanding contribution to the music industry at the World Music Awards, singing the appropriately titled "I Don't Want to Fight" at the ceremony.

In May, she appeared on the Tonight Show and sang the song again on the BBC show Top of the Pops. In June, she embarked on her first North American concert tour in six years, beginning in Reno, Nevada, and including Fleetwood Mac's Lindsey Buckingham, who was eventually replaced for the second leg of the tour by Chris Isaak. While she was on the road doing what she does best, the film debuted as a massive box office success, drawing even more attention to her turbulent past. She had to be wondering when she would no longer have to talk about Ike Turner, having already created an Ikeless future for herself.

As she always did, she told friends who knew the backstory that it was difficult not only to see the story of her life filmed in that manner, but also to cope with the resurgence of primal energies associated with her relationship, which is why I believe she has been so adeptly managing posttraumatic stress for years. She reasoned that getting it out of her system would be equivalent to no longer hiding the agony, to letting the world know her by allowing them into her genuine tale. At first, it appeared that no one understood her decisions, but it soon became evident that they, and we, were.

She had always felt that Ike's weird way of believing he dominated others via sex was what wrecked him, but that was obviously not what kept her in the terrible relationship. It was her great feeling of loyalty, rather. Another profound regret she has is that the film did not depict her entire complex story, inventive early career growth, or family connections. In fact, considering how bad her personal story was, the Disney business worried that audiences would never accept that there were some (many) happy moments as well.

"What else was I supposed to do?" She asked Hirshey for her history of soul music. I had to go to work. So I worked." Essentially, the film is the narrative of a woman locked in a nightmarish relationship who must be both a mother and a professional, meeting as many commitments as she can at the same time. The picture was a box office success and received mainly excellent reviews: the Los Angeles Times, Entertainment Weekly, and the Chicago Sun-Times all agreed it was one of the best 10 films of the year.

The Sun-Times' Roger Ebert called it "one of the most harrowing, uncompromising showbiz biographies I've ever seen." It contains a lot of great music, but it's not your usual showbiz musical. It's a story of sorrow and courage, unflinchingly honest and unflinchingly honest, and the next time I hear Tina Turner sing, I'll listen to the song in a whole new manner." Most of us will, too. "What's love got to do with it?" wondered Rita Kempley of the Washington Post. I'm afraid there isn't much. It's a shady but savage biopic with a weave of rhythm and blues and a weft of beatings. The next thing you know, she's shouting 'Proud Mary,' and Ike's belting her. The film, like the couple's co-dependent relationship, is aggressively acted out and blazing with spectacular production numbers."
WHAT HAS LOVE TO DO WITH IT? (VIRGIN RECORDS-PARLOPHONE)

It was released in 1993. Chris Lord, Rupert Hine, Bryan Adams, Terry Britten, and Robert "Mutt" Lange produced the album. Tina Turner (vocals); Laurence Fishburne (spoken vocal on "It's Gonna Work Out Fine"); James Ralston (guitar and vocals); Gene Black and Keith Scott (guitars); Tommy Cappello (saxophones); Lee Thornburg (trumpet); David Paitch (piano); C. J. Vanston on keyboards, Rupert Hine on keyboards, Bob Feit on bass, Robbie King on Hammond organ, Trevor Morais on drums, Simon Morton on percussion, and Tuck Back Twins on vocals. Chris Lord-Alge, Steve McNamara, John Hudson, and Doug Sax worked as engineers. The video lasts 51:52 minutes.

Touchstone Pictures released her ninth studio album as the soundtrack to the film of the same name. Turner re recorded many of her earlier Ike and Tina Turner songs, including their first single together, "A Fool in Love," as well as a vampy version of the Trammps disco classic hit "Disco Inferno," one of her favorite songs to perform live in the late 1970s. Two songs from her Private Dancer CD were also featured.

This album debuted at number one in the United Kingdom (as is customary for Tina) and was certified platinum in other countries. Tina's version of "You Know I Love You" is not the same as the BB King song she famously initially sung with Ike as a teenager; hers is a slightly different more rock version written with her bandmates for this soundtrack, though she still acknowledges BB King with the title.

I Don't Wanna Fight (Lulu, Billy Lawrie, Steve DuBerry) 6:06 / Rock Me Baby 93 Version (Riley King, Joe Josea) 3:57 / Disco Inferno (Leroy Green, Ron Kersey) 4:03 / Why Must We Wait Until Tonight (Bryan Adams, Robert Lange) 5:53 / Stay Awhile (Terry Britten, Graham Lyle)

CHAPTER 8:
BETTER THAN THE OTHERS

Aside from putting on headphones and listening to the recorded artifacts they left behind, one of the finest methods to study a musical artist's social and cultural impact is to research the visual archive of videos they bestowed in order to both document and advertise their songs. This is especially true for a performer as photogenic and dynamic as Tina Turner, whose second coming of age coincided with the birth and explosion of televised music videos at precisely the right historical moment for them to fully capture and capitalize on her style and substance.

It was a medium tailor-made for Tina's showy persona, and she, like many other large-scale performers, would gain greatly from it while also revolutionizing it as an artistic form of expression. Her brilliant videos, which she produced in droves, were National Geographic documentaries of the devotion she wore on her sleeve or, rather, on her skirt. Her voice, features, and even her legs were perfectly suited to the flamboyant swagger that videos so viscerally celebrate.

Tina Turner's debut videos arrived just in time to catch this new wave while it was in full swing and also to define its future bounds with her particular sense of style, and she has often called her concerts itself as "small movies."

Even more than in her ostensibly straight acting parts in big-budget films, we see concrete and tactile evidence of her irresistible appeal in her music videos. They are the epitome of scopophilia.

Aside from Madonna, Cher, and Michael Jackson, few music stars have matched Turner's raw theatrical impact on film, despite the fact that her videos featured no special effects or grandiose production gimmicks. She was her very own special effect. They were deceptively simple and basic: Tina standing or, more often, strolling and simply delivering the song. Her movies frequently feel like private diary entries given in a startlingly intimate manner.

After an artist has passed away, taking their magical aura with them, and independent of their followers' memories of seeing them live or hearing their recordings, their films are frequently the sole historical document that can be consulted in order to examine their theater skill. From my perspective, the ideal way to approach this exercise in appreciation is for the reader, listener, or viewer to evaluate this brief handpicked selection.

To get a sense of her raw power, start with the easily available classic 1970-1971 performances Tina did with the Revue on the Ed Sullivan Show delivering "River Deep, Mountain High" and "Proud Mary." Then shift gears slightly and get a sense of her depth by watching what she was capable of later on in the videos she produced after she had become a lauded solo artist and consummate pop star. Several films show glimpses of some of her distinctive performing strategies, such as her strategy of appearing to be seemingly effortless despite decades of hard preparation.

Here's a quick taster. But who exactly are we seeing in all of these videos? Aside from being an obviously otherworldly creature, she's also a performer who doesn't require much artificial or glittery sparkle to hook us on. Her strategy is almost shockingly simple: sing the song—and sing it so authentically that we often miss the fact that she's lip-syncing the tune in the middle of city streets. What is her name? To this day, he remains a mystery.

But it comes to me that in these songs and videos, she is admitting her sentiments. Even more startling, she is still testifying in the traditional sense, but she is now doing so in a gospel-funk manner: she is no longer worshiping at any altar—she has become the altar.

In retrospect, it is very evident that she was employing an exceptional survival mechanism through her work as a performer. By bearing her soul, she was bearing her life. Another of her performance secrets seemed to be obvious to me as well. She reminds me of one of our own Swiftian humorist George Burns' stage lectures and the wise advice he offered to artists everywhere: the most important thing you need is authenticity; if you can fake that, you've got it made. She was also so genuine that you couldn't see a speck of the underlying deception that had to be there. And it's in her music videos that her lack of deception is most evident. Turner appeared in a number of excellent ones, but her greatest are almost classically intimate self-portraits.

DAVID MALLET'S "BALL OF CONFUSION," 1982: 3:50

Originally a Temptations soul ballad and successful single, Tina Turner covered it for volume 1 of the Music for Quality and Distinction series in 1982, incorporating a very early modern synthesizer backing. It charted remarkably well in Europe and was republished on CD in 1991 in a remixed version as well as in her boxed collection of collected recordings, but the single was never released in the United States. This would be Turner's debut song with a music video, filmed live on stage with her female dancers and musicians; nevertheless, the music came from a tape with Tina lip-syncing the words. Mallett, who went on to direct several of her most famous videos, also incorporated special effects like stop-action animation and slow motion. Tina made history in this video by becoming one of the first black musicians to appear on MTV when the network expanded its programming. It was never officially released on DVD.

"WHAT DOES LOVE HAVE TO DO WITH IT?DIRECTED BY MARK ROBINSON IN 1983: 3:47

Tina's first number one success in the United States and the single released to promote Tina's album Private Dancer, the song won two Grammy Awards in 1985. There are two video versions. The first, directed by John Caldwell, is in black and white and rather sad, featuring Tina close up with bare shoulders as various couples behind her engage in an awkward manner. At the end, she ascends a spiral staircase in a leather gown, her eyes displayed in extreme close-up, leaving an overall impression of grief, which may explain why it was rarely shown on television.

Tina was filmed live in New York City wearing a jean jacket and a black miniskirt in the second version, which was produced by Bud Schaetzle and has a significantly different visual tone and emotional mood. The song progresses till the end, as she stops at a graffiti chalk depiction of the Private Dancer album cover image, while looking at the East River, then emerging from a subway station, going down bustling public streets, and mingling with others. The video was nominated for an MTV Music Award and is also included on the Simply the Best DVD.

"BETTER BE GOOD TO ME," DIRECTED BY BRIAN GRANT IN 1983: 4:03

This fourth single from Private Dancer was a rock song originally performed by Spider from the United States, and it earned Turner her third solo Grammy Award for vocal performance in 1985. Adrian Irving directed the song video, which was shot at the Beverly Theater in Los Angeles in 1984, while Tina was on tour with Lionel Ritchie. The auditorium was packed with admirers attracted from advertisements and her gigs to stage a concert specifically for the filming, in which she donned racy slacks and a leather jacket with her band, which included Jamie West-Oram, guitarist for the British rock band Fixx. Toni Basil choreographed a betrayal scenario in which Cy Curnin plays Turner's wicked lover.

This footage was first released on the Private Dancer EP in a shorter version, while a longer version includes more of Curnin's cameo appearance. The American music magazine Cashbox reported in July 1984 that a further video for "I Might Have Been Queen" was shot at the same location, albeit the song was never issued as a single. They cited her distinctive gruff sassiness as evidence of her unrivaled status as rock's first lady in their judgment. "'Better Be Good to Me' grinds with a menacing beat that rolls and charges forward with Turner's energized vocal"—not to mention her extremely tight shining black leather trousers.

5:25 in "PRIVATE DANCER," directed by Brian Grant in 1983.
The title tune and sixth single from Private Dancer, produced by Pam Grant, is staged as a substantial pop ballad. This is the song Turner claims she had no idea was about a high-class prostitute. Because corporation advertising is not permitted in the United Kingdom, the lyric referring to American Express was changed to mention the

British currency of pounds sterling, although all other commercial releases include the original line regarding American Express.

The video was shot at the Rialto Theater in Lewisham, London, and shows Turner as a "hostess" looking fatigued and pale as she dances with a man in a dance hall until she begins to dream. She goes through various fantasy scenes, looking pretty lovely in a dazzling sequined gown, until she wakes up and recognizes her sad reality, turning away from her dance partner and fleeing the room. A lengthier version with an additional instrumental section and an extended introduction was also created.

It's as if her entire comeback decade was documented on tape in real time. In fact, it sometimes appears that the whole 1980s era occurred solely on television. James Porter pondered the subject of why the mid-1980s seemed to be the perfect time for Tina's resurgence with his customary clarity. "Everyone enjoys a good bad-luck story. Even more, everyone enjoys seeing someone recover from adversity. Tina was the Comeback Queen from 1984 to 1985. I recall reading articles on earlier rock and roll musicians, and they'd always include a reference to Tina, almost as if to say, if Tina Turner can do it, so can I! Even better, her return was permanent."

Tina's qualities as a visionary trendsetter were also lauded by Porter. "Tina has frequently claimed that the transition to a rockier sensibility was her idea. This is supported by the fact that she has been moving in that direction since the beginning of her solo career. She wasn't attempting to compete with Anita Baker, Shirley Murdock, Whitney Houston, Gwen Guthrie, or fellow veteran Patti La-Belle with her string of comeback singles in the 1980s. Listening to those songs now, she sounds like a less acoustic high-tech ancestor to Melissa Etheridge or Sheryl Crow. While Tina's legacy as an R&B icon should not be diminished, she deserves to be recognized as one of the first black female rockers, predating everyone from Betty Davis to Nikki Hill.

"When most performers return from nowhere, they appear for a year and then vanish." Tina remained in the forefront thanks to a new age of hits. It's difficult to explain why the timing was so perfect for her.

During the so-called Cosby decade, following Michael Jackson's popularity, white America was amenable to black musicians with just enough of a pop sheen: Lionel Richie comes to mind, and to a lesser extent Billy Ocean.

"Tina Turner, survivor of a disastrous marriage and an almost-failed career, could have been caught up in this wave." The difference was that Tina, like Prince, had an openly rock image, which was uncommon among major black musicians in the mid-1980s. Lionel Richie was more pop, aiming for the middle ground with preppy attire and a nice-guy persona. Tina, even in the sophisticated United Kingdom. production, she never lost her sexy rock mama persona. And she could do it with impeccable taste."

Similarly, I asked Aaron Cohen if he thought anything about her character made her a distinct kind of heroine, one who was well matched to the peculiar traits of our period and culture, particularly in the 1980s. "Her willingness to take chances, her seemingly open perspective, and her sheer endurance would make her a heroine for any time and culture." Indeed, and for me, a large part of her heroism was her capacity to share all of herself with us, especially her most vulnerable bits.

Tina Turner has openly admitted that when she was experiencing her freedom for the first time after liberating herself from her cultish first marriage, back when she had no money to speak of and plenty of time to kill, she made her fair share of mistakes with men—none as big as her first huge one, of course, and probably no different than anyone else who was searching, experimenting, and maybe ev I'm very sure her initial independence included some form of therapy, whether self-applied through her chanting or professional in nature, such as a talking cure.

Perhaps her preparation for the blockbuster biographical film about her life and music was also a type of talking cure, perhaps geared to aid in the deprogramming required when someone escapes from a cult. But then Erwin Bach appeared, as a sort of human solution. By all accounts a self-assured but timid and retiring guy who was accomplished in his own right, he didn't seek any attention or spotlight for himself; in fact, he seemed to shun it like the plague, and he was very content to let all the cameras focus on his girlfriend. Erwin appeared pleased to let her be admired in public while adoring her privately.

"I finally got involved with a man who cared about me," she explained to Harper's. "I even had trouble getting a relationship out of him, because he didn't want a high-profile life." He's starting to accept this way of life now." One of her particular qualities, which she seemed to share with Bach, was how their separation of business (especially his) and professional (especially hers) and personal (especially theirs) lives was a solid approach. Their relationship has nothing to do with employment, which is a wise decision considering the well-known risks of going the other route.

One obvious life lesson she learned from her early experiences was to never mix the business and private sides of her activities again, as she had when her husband was also her manager, musical partner, producer, and spouse, especially since her new love was already a music executive with EMI at the start of their romantic alliance together. She knew that was the path to insanity.

She also has little time for the idea of retirement, despite the fact that her publicly known health concerns have clearly limited much of her public barnstorming. She might entertain the thought of retirement very frequently, possibly as a vague, abstract term, and she did make a halfhearted try once or twice, but the concept never seemed to suit her temperament.

On April 13, 1999, VH1 persuaded the then-mostly-calm pop singer to take another break from silence in order to star in its second-annual Divas Live TV special—not only to star, but also to begin the entire extravaganza as the show's lead act. Faith Hill, Cher, Chaka Khan, Mary J. Blige, and Whitney Houston were among the other so-called divas (a term that originally meant goddess or divine creature, rather than simply a prima donna). Perhaps Diana Ross and Barbra Streisand were unable due to scheduling conflicts.

A couple of teenage diva students, Brandy and Leanne Rimes, were also invited, as was a special kind of diva all his own, Elton John, to symbolize a kind of reverse distaff side for the particular event. That's a lot of diva energy gathered in one spot at once. On March 23, Polygram Records had just issued Elton's most recent CD, his personal interpretation on the famous opera Aida, on which Tina had sung a song called "Easy as Life," and they were also in talks about a new project they'd both work on later in the year.

Everything appeared to be on track until, during a full rehearsal, the two divas clashed in an emotional scream-fest, prompting Elton to run from the stage to his dressing trailer, followed by Tina, where they engaged in another mysterious screamfest before Elton returned to the rehearsal and apologized to Turner in front of all the other musicians. The planned concert tour that year was abruptly shelved and subsequently canceled.

Despite this little bump in their path, the Divas Live show was an enormous televised hit concert event, with the two of them doing that ironic duet together on his quirky song "The Bitch Is Back." After wowing the crowd, Tina chortled, "Wow, divas and bitches, my goodness." Their follow-up number was an even more raucous barnstormer, "Proud Mary," a song Tina introduced as being about the oldest diva of them all. They were joined in the midst of the song by another singer with comparable diva-wattage, Cher, and the three of them rode the tune home in a beautiful vehicle of delicious ham at its finest.

But, like with most years in this star's tumultuous existence, 1999 was a bizarre mix of pleasure and anguish, victory and tragedy. Her mother, Zelma, who never showed her any affection and abandoned her as soon as she could, died in October of that year at the age of eighty-one (the same age Tina is at the time of this writing). The potentially irreconcilable difficulties in their convoluted relationship would remain unresolved forever, and while I'm no psychologist, I believe Tina's own traumas of abandonment contributed to her unwillingness to ever abandon her first husband, despite everything he did to her. She had been hardwired, so to speak, to remain loyal long after it was in her best interests to do so.

She had attempted to bridge the gap between herself and Zelma, knowing that her mother had clearly benefited from her loud daughter's global fame, but without any maternal success. "She ended up living in a very nice big house, being very respected and recognized as 'Tina Turner's mother,' and her last days were her best," she told People magazine. My mother never really knew me, and she always attributed my success to Ike. There was a chasm between us because she never imagined it was me.``

Tina's mother and elder sister Alline (who died in 2010 at the age of seventy-three) never seemed to accept her for her evident brilliance, with Tina telling Us magazine that "we were two separate people but Ike took all the credit, they thought he did everything." They weren't even aware that I was important. I eventually took Ma to Paris, London, Switzerland, and New York to show her the world, and she still didn't believe I had done anything for myself."

Tina chose not to attend her mother's funeral so that she would not be the center of attention on that special day. Besides, Ike was there, just out of jail and signing autographs from his vehicle window, and she wasn't going to share space with him again. So, fresh from that grieving experience, Tina did what she usually did best to alleviate her suffering: she returned to work.

Throughout 1999, she was working on her next album, Twenty Four Seven, as well as the ensuing global tour. The album was her signature fusion of pop and heavier rock, with plenty of contributions from fellow stars who had all become steadfast collaborators by this point, including Terry Britten, the Gibb brothers, and Bryan Adams, among others.

TWENTY-SEVEN (VIRGIN RECORDS)

It was released in 1999. Johnny Douglas, Terry Britten, Brian Rawling, and Mark Taylor produced. Tina Turner on vocals; Bryan Adams on vocals; Pete Lincoln on acoustic guitar; Pino Palladino on bass; Peter Hope-Evans on harmonica; Duncan Mackay, Mike Stevens, Nichol Thompson on horns; Mark Taylor on keyboards;

London Musicians Orchestra on strings; Steve Sidwell on trumpet. Mark Lane, Ren Swan, and Paul Wright worked as engineers. Doug Stax is in charge of mastering. Time taken: 47:09.

Whatever You Need (Harriet Roberts) 4:49 / All the Woman (Paul Wilson) 4:03 / When the Heartache Is Over (Graham Stack) 3:44 / Absolutely Nothing's Changed (Terry Britten, John O'Kane) 3:43 / Talk to My Heart (Johnny Douglas, Graham Lyle) 5:08 / Don't Leave Me This Way (Paul Barry) 4:19

True to her words to an audience at one of her final Wildest Dreams gigs, she returned three years later with her tenth studio album, as well as the final record and concert tour before her first of multiple announced retirements. This final album was created by the same team that worked on Cher's blockbuster Believe, among other things. Another parallel, following the same kind of arrival at a similarly lofty pop peak shared by both Cher and Madonna, the album cover this time required only her single, first name to identify the star: Tina.

"Twenty-four seven found Turner in an upbeat, adult, contemporary kind of mood," wrote Jane Stevenson of the Toronto Sun. "This collection came together following Turner and Cher's knockout performances at last year's VH 1 Divas show, in which they both wiped the floor with Elton John, Brandy, and Whitney Houston." They both had also not joined the all-cast finale version of Houston's epic "I'm Every Woman" for reasons that have often been speculated about but never clearly defined.

"Gone is the grit of the music she made with former husband Ike," Paul Elliot of Q magazine commented on the album. ...Tina Turner is still regarded as a true superstar fifteen years after making the most unexpected comeback of the 1980s. "These eleven tracks of grown-up pop should keep business running smoothly." It did, indeed, keep running.

Tina Turner celebrated her sixtieth birthday in the final year of the twentieth century (it's hard to believe she turned eighty in 2019 as I write these words), and naturally, the best way she could think of to celebrate her sixty years on earth was to stage a gala concert in London.

Of course, it was also filmed and published on DVD as The Best of Tina Turner: Celebrate! And, predictably, she sang a mix of her biggest hits—"River Deep" and "What's Love," of course—along with songs from her most recent album, Twenty Four Seven, including "When the Heartache Is Over," "Whatever You Need," and the touching ballad "Talk to My Heart," dedicated to her late mother. When asked about the impact of her sixtieth year, she told People magazine, "it's just mental." She then went on to celebrate the upcoming millennium with a massive concert show in Las Vegas, immediately followed by the release of her new record in America in January, and on January 30, she performed both "Proud Mary," by then a kind of private anthem, and "When the Heartache Is Over," by then a kind of secular hymn, at the Super Bowl.

After her record was released worldwide, she embarked on another 116-city tour, beginning in Minneapolis and concluding in Anaheim, during which she declared that this would be her final tour, leading tickets to sell out in a feeding frenzy. This is one astute lady. "I've never worked out at all," she told Rolling Stone of how she managed to maintain the energy to be a rock-and-roll dynamo at her age. I'm a country girl who has had a full country life, which I believe has made me strong."

Apart from All the Best in 2004, Tina: The Platinum Collection in 2008, Love Songs in 2014, and The Greatest Hits in 2018, this would be Turner's final recording. There were some surprises in store for fans, however: a series of non-pop CDs with Buddhist and interfaith content that demonstrated her shifting gears once more. She had promised a few years before that she would eventually give up pop and rock music and focus on spiritual pursuits and lectures. However, her party train continued to roll.

On December 6, 2000, she performed at the Arrowhead Auditorium in Anaheim, near downtown Los Angeles, to a raucous sold-out crowd of 18,000 writhing and shouting fans who could have been at a Beatles concert. According to the Hollywood Reporter, "Tina

Turner, 61, took in $80 million in ticket sales for 95 concerts," and was the biggest grossing concert draw of the whole first year of the twenty-first century, according to Pollster.

Her incredible performance at Wembley Stadium in London was captured on tape and released as One Last Time in Concert, and you definitely have to see how she charmed the crowd next to her backup dancers (her flowers), each of whom was roughly a third her age. She is really incredible.

Sure enough, four years later, Hollywood buzzed around her like a bee around a flower, this time potentially in an even more exotic and over-the-top character than her Mad Max Aunty Entity turn. Tina Turner was in talks with Merchant Ivory Productions in 2004 to play the lead part in The Goddess, a film about the Indian deity Kali/Shakti, a feminine divinity of destruction, fertility, and renewal. "Famous for power-packed musical performances in high heels and leather miniskirts, the 64-year-old singer would star as the Hindu symbol for female power and energy in a film being planned by Indian-Anglo duo Ismail Merchant and James Ivory, best known for their series of lavish period pieces."

The announcement sparked an immediate backlash in the orthodox Hindu community, with many calling her participation a "outrage" and claiming in mass protests that her reputation as a "sex icon" disqualified her from the role—which is somewhat ironic given that Shakti also represents creative energy and, more specifically, feminine sexuality, in keeping with the dualist principles at work in Hindu philosophy.

Ismail Merchant responded in the Times of India, saying that religious groups' protests were based on "misconceptions about the film," which were actually made in a "spirit of reverence." He added, "Tina Turner is one of the great artists of our time and has also been a practicing Buddhist for the last twenty years, an artist of such international stature should be welcomed."

Given the vocal criticism, it's difficult not to compare this picture to Doom with a View, yet Merchant seems to have his heart set on it despite the obvious challenges. He attempted to clarify his and her viewpoints by mentioning that they had been to India together in preparation for the collaborative endeavor, hoping to experience some of the many cultural and spiritual beauties that the country has to offer. He went on to explain to the worried religious community that their story would be based in part on a tale from the Kathasaritasagara, a vast repository of folktales, and would take place in ancient India.

"Contrary to the accusations of the objectors," Merchant stated in a Merchant Ivory news release intended to calm the uproar, "nobody is going to sing and dance on the back of a tiger, the Goddess is not going to be half-naked, or a sex symbol." She is not intended to be a specific portrayal of any one deity, whether it is Kail, Laxmi, or Druga. Instead, she is Shakti, the universal feminine spirit manifested in Kali, Druga, Mother Mary, Wicca, and every woman in the world."

Merchant made a gallant but futile attempt to assert that no one has the authority to prescribe how one should worship the Goddess or to discriminate against an artist who wishes to depict Her. "The Goddess extends her compassion and wisdom to everyone, whether Hindu, Muslim, Christian, or atheist." A true devotee should join us in celebrating a film that will disseminate Devi's life-affirming message all over the world." He also expressed hope that the majority would not be persuaded by a few fanatics attempting to create a crisis where none exists. "I am encouraged in this hope because all Hindus understand its central message: all creation is one family."

Meanwhile, the Independent noted Turner's typically upbeat attitude about all of her potential projects: "The cosmic energy of Shakti attracted me to this film and the film to me." It represents new beginnings." Unfortunately, many were convinced by the minority viewpoint, and a few health difficulties that began to arise in Turner's life at the time may have further complicated the planned partnership. There has been no trace of the tough and engaging film about communal sharing manifesting in the actual world to this day.

However, one other significant component of Turner's past did appear to concretely manifest in her life later on. After all, she would play the role of goddess in her own unique way. It was part of her private romantic life, and it was also something she had said she would never do again: she was going to incorporate a new husband into her ongoing fiction. Marriage was reclaiming itself in a unique way and after a lengthy time of waiting on the part of the groom: her long-term companion, lover, friend, and partner, Erwin Bach.

Bach, a German music producer, actor, and managing director of EMI Music in Switzerland, was born on January 24, 1956, around the time that sixteen-year-old Anna Mae Bullock began secretly watching the Kings of Rhythm perform their sizzling boogie-blues music at the Club Manhattan in East St. Louis with her elder sister Alline. There is some misunderstanding regarding how Bach and Turner met.

According to most sources, they initially met at an EMI record label party in 1985, almost nine years after her first husband filed for divorce. She was still fragile enough to be concerned about future love affairs. But she was also courageous enough to reveal them. No one could ever describe them as accurately or candidly as she did in her memories of late but true romance, which she would share in her Davis-curated memories dubbed My Love Story.

"The wig is an essential component of Tina Turner's look." If I stepped onstage with my natural hair, the audience would not know me and would ask, "Where is Tina?"'I've always thought of it as an extension of myself. I'll never get rid of the wig. I was always afraid of meeting a man who would oppose becoming intimately associated with Tina, with her abundant hair and gorgeous decorations, but waking up with plain Anna Mae. What if the real me disappointed him? I was always a little hesitant to take that risk."

That is, until the fateful day when she and manager Roger Davies flew into Cologne to prepare for a busy run of gigs on the Private Dancer Tour in 1984-1985. As they entered, a young man emerged from behind some columns to meet them. She initially mistook him for a fan, but Roger recognized him immediately and cordially greeted him with "Hello Erwin." He reached his arms out and said, "Hello." She took a few steps back because she didn't know who he was. Then came the formal introductions, and Turner found herself excessively drawn to this "unusually handsome" man.

She later reported that her heart was racing when they got into the car together. But, as she recalls, that was never a major issue because she was so preoccupied with the tour at the time that she never had time for a boyfriend, no matter how attractive. Touring had been a way of life for the enormously popular entertainer, who had always been a continual energy performer on the road since her youth, but this time she was truly loving it, despite the fact that it left little to no time for much of a personal life.

But it wasn't the fancy Mercedes vehicle he'd brought for her to surprise her, but rather the man himself. "Apparently, the keys in this charismatic stranger's hand were to my heart, which suddenly began to beat loudly and drown out all other sounds." All I could think was, "Oh my God, I'm not prepared for this!'"It didn't matter if he was younger or lived in Europe. I believe I require love. I was a free woman with the ability to choose. And I went with Erwin."

Furthermore, in keeping with her Buddhist religion, she stated in her Love Story that she was confident they had been together before in another life, and she has also addressed the obvious elephant in the room from the public's perspective: the age difference. She acknowledged that, although the rest of the world saw him as "Tina's younger man," she believed he was sixty and she was sixteen. "It was time for me to take care of myself."

And, much to her surprise and delight, a significant part of taking care of herself in that way also included allowing Erwin take care of her (once she grew weak enough with her health issues to let him) in order to convey the actual degree of his affection for her. He apparently persuaded her into allowing him to do so as well, just as he had charmed her sister and stern mother when they eventually met him. He even went so far as to eventually woo her into accepting his compassionate donation of one of his own kidneys when it was later proven crucial for her survival, as the world now knows.

Yes, this was certainly a case of love at first sight. He needed a little more convincing, but they were dating soon enough; in fact, they dated for the next twenty-seven years. The relationship just grew stronger over time. He was a continuous source of support for her and assisted her with her children. Bach proposed to Turner at least twice more over the years until they married in July 2013 in Zurich, where they now live.

Turner has repeatedly described him as a man who made her dizzy when she first saw him. He proposed to her for the first time in 1989, three years after they'd been together as life partners. She was fifty at the time, and he was thirty-one; she knew how she felt about him but had been reasonably wary of marriage for years. Her reaction was a kind acknowledgement that she didn't yet have an answer to the inquiry. So, according to all accounts, he waited a couple of decades before proposing again, this time while traveling around the Mediterranean on a friend's yacht.

She accepted this time; she was seventy-three years old, and in her young mind, she was getting married for the first time because the first try as a twenty-one-year-old had not been quite what it appeared to be at the time. Besides, her first husband took her to a brothel on their wedding night, which started a long nightmare for her. This one was more of a fairy tale, unfolding in a floating castle, the Chateau Algonquin just outside of Zurich, where Bach had been working for the previous fifteen years, almost as if in destiny compensation for everything she'd been through.

They arrived at the wedding site in a black Rolls-Royce convertible to the sound of what Tina must have thought of as a type of theme song for her: Frank Sinatra's "My Way" ("The record shows, I took the blows and did it my way"). Bryan Adams, her musical buddy and regular album collaborator, provided the walking-down-the-aisle music, crooning his ballad "All for Love" ("Let's make it all for one and all for love").

The completely stupid yet romantically perfect spectacle done by Bach and about fifteen of his buddies dressed in Mexican sombreros serenading the gathering with strange mariachi music was in the air, she felt. She was having the time of her life after working extraordinarily hard during extremely difficult times, all on her own and without assistance from anyone. She is undoubtedly entitled to believe that her life was blessed at the time, and she even articulated her essentially Buddhist notion: this must be my nirvana.

But 2013 was far from a sunny nirvana-fest. Three months later, she awoke with severe aches in her brain and legs, barely able to shout out for aid to her new husband, caught hopelessly in the midst of a catastrophic stroke. The next thing she knew (or thought she knew) was that she was hooked up to a lifesaving dialysis machine in a hospital in Zollikon, not far from where she lives, with only 20% kidney function and the need to become physically strong enough to accept a critical surgical transplant.

Years of high blood pressure, probably undiagnosed or untreated, had harmed her kidneys, which were now exacerbated by her stroke. Bach had carefully guarded their privacy for several years, tending to his wife's treatments and keeping everything on track during her sessions to have her blood "washed." Undergoing these rigors prompted Turner to do two things: look at every day through the clarifying lens of impermanence, to which her Buddhism already inclined her, and also reflect on her good fortune in meeting the true love of her life.

The sight of Tina Turner smiling while linked to her life-saving medical machine and shared with the globe is rather startling. Only the down-to-earth yet typically fantastically glamorous Tina would have the courage or honesty to communicate what she was going through with so many people who cared about her at this time in her life, which was already outstanding by anyone's standards. Without a question, the lady has guts.

She was often amused when people asked her "what do you do now that you're retired?" following her triumphant new millennium tours. because she had always assumed that was the entire point: you don't do anything anymore, you just live. When people who loom so large on the public stage retire into private relaxation, their admirers begin to believe they've already died, a notion she dispelled by emerging from her seclusion in 2005 to be honored alongside Cher and Tony Bennett at the Kennedy Center Awards for contributions to American culture. She even had the distinct pleasure of not only being seen and worshiped again, but also of witnessing Beyoncé perform a spirit-lifting rendition of her signature song (or one of them), "Proud Mary," knowing full well that it was great dames like herself who made artists like Beyoncé possible.

Her so-called solitude was, of course, far from lonely or immovable, not least because she was touring the world with her ex-Erwin and indulged in one of her favorite hobbies: adorning her homes with art and design treasures. She'd spent the last few years calmly planning, arranging, and preparing, confidently structuring the reasons for her retirement, downsizing, and commitment to focusing on what was actually essential. She was regaining complete control of her life. Do you know the saying, "If you want to make God laugh, just tell him your plans?" That was her wistful take on it.

In retrospect, she must have thought she heard the creator's laughter, because "control" was not a word that could be applied to her current situation. One solution to the public issue of what you do after you're retired could be that survival, like being righteous, is sometimes a full-time job. She was hit with the primitive anxiety that comes with immobility after being wheeled into the hospital, which was a shock for someone used to strutting so spectacularly.

The strange concept that Tina Turner might ever be immobilized was especially daunting for someone used to commanding her stallion-like body to perform her bidding. Dr. Vetter, her doctor, described how the stroke had affected her so severely. Her entire right side was numb, and she'd need physiotherapy to learn to walk again, let alone swagger.

She was hospitalized for about 10 days, during which time she did what Tina Turner would do: she talked herself into believing she could battle her way back to health.

One major concern was that the news and the accompanying public chatter would become fuel for whisperings all around the world: Tina Turner has a secret illness, Tina Turner is recovering from a stroke, is Tina Turner still alive, and so on. She tried to block out all negative thoughts and concentrate on her recuperation, which had been a protracted process involving acupuncture, traditional Chinese medicine, meditation, and chanting, her own unique form of prayer.

The physical consequences of the stroke lasted a long time. Even five years later, in 2018, she still struggled with facial muscles, getting up, walking, and even penning her name. That's when her doctor told her depressed patient that her high blood pressure, either caused by the stroke or simply dormant for years, was affecting kidney function, which had now risen to a still-low 35%. She was referred to a nephrologist, Dr. Jorg Bleisch, who required frequent monitoring and began prescribing intense blood pressure medicine.

The severe vertigo set in, and she was referred to Dominick Straumann, a neurologist at a prestigious Swiss research institute who administered treatments to correct her otoconia, a loosening of crystals in the ear canal that causes dizziness. The procedures, which were more physically and intellectually demanding than anything she had ever encountered, were gradually but steadily taking effect. "How did I go from being the picture of health, a cover girl, and a bride, for God's sake, to being Job?" she asked in her Love Story reminiscences, referring to the biblical character who was forced to suffer so many painful tests and threatening tribulations.

Then, in a dramatic case of one awful thing after another, her kidneys failed her completely, unable to execute their duty of removing waste from the body and jeopardizing their host, the person they purportedly "belong" to. Someone else's kidney may have to be found in this scenario for a renal transplant, when at least one completely functioning kidney can do the job of two. Historically, kidney transplant patients live substantially longer than those who continue on dialysis treatment, and they have a far higher quality of life while doing so.

Then, in January 2016, while adjusting to the thought of recuperation, therapy, and transplantation, and being forced to accept, to some extent, the limitations of being an invalid, Turner was shocked to learn that she had been diagnosed with intestinal cancer. She had a carcinoma with multiple malignant polyps, which necessitated a variety of surgical operations and further treatments. This appeared to be one of those last-straw situations, forcing even Tina to feel dejected enough to ask her husband Erwin if he was sorry he had married an elderly woman.

Apart from meeting him in the first place, she could be glad for the fact that she was gradually realizing that he was not a typical man. His optimism, love of life, and love for her seemed to shine through and bring her up and over the few bad times, including her operation only a month after the diagnosis, during which part of her intestine was removed and cellular development was hoped to be arrested. However, the cancer's and surgery's attacks on her immune system were simultaneously weakening her renal system and her already impaired kidneys.

She was defying her doctors' efforts to encourage her to continue dialysis. Being a woman in her seventies with cancer and, to put it mildly, a considerable strength of character, she rejected the thought of living forever hooked to a machine out of hand. Instead, she bravely began researching end-of-life options such as assisted suicide and supportive suicide, and even joined an organization called Exit just in case. Another Swiss organization called Dignitas was also available to her if she needed to take the last stages.

Her companion Erwin, on the other hand, vowed that he would give her one of his own kidneys. She tried to persuade him to think about his own future, given his younger age, but he said that their future was his future, giving her the hope she sorely needed to continue with the full-time task of survival. His point of view, which was not lost on his Buddhist wife, was that giving was equally a gift to the donor. He thought that if you gave, you will receive. One more time, the unexpected concept of karma rears its hopeful head in her life.

So, for the following nine months, the dialysis chair at the clinic would become not just the center of her existence, but also the center of their universe. Their joint kidney transplant was set for April 7, 2017. She passed the time by recalling memories, reading her favorite spiritual literature, using homeopathic treatments, and meditating and chanting, but largely by being three people at once: Anna Mae Bullock, Tina Turner, and Mrs. Erwin Bach.

Following what appeared to be a medically successful transplant, her husband kept her busy, understanding that the best way to help his wife would be to help her continue to be Tina Turner, the lady he'd fallen in love with nearly thirty years before. He invited approximately ten people into their home one day to discuss a creative project they had all been working on: a Broadway musical theater performance called Tina: The Tina Turner Musical, which would tell the story of her life in song, dance, and drama live on stage.

She must have understood after some convincing and cajoling that this theatrical spectacle was something destined to be, so with her typical resignation in the face of fate (her fate, that is), she agreed to give it her blessing. Her plan was to become fit enough to attend the theater group's official announcement of the show's development on October 18, 2017, at which time they would also introduce the talented young actress chosen to play Tina: Adrienne Warren.

Six months after her major organ transplant, her body appeared to be on the verge of rejecting Erwin's gifted kidney, and she wondered if she'd be in good enough shape to do what she eventually did, as if by sheer force of willpower: dress up as Tina Turner once more and join young Adrienne onstage at the launch reception to sing "Proud Mary" together. She appeared to be the living embodiment of a major existential principle: I can't go on, but I will.

Six months later, in April 2018, the Tina Turner Musical made its formal debut at the Aldwych, one of London's oldest functioning theaters. When the event began with the first number, "Nutbush City Limits," she understood she was in for a genuinely bizarre encounter. Warren and the actor hired to play her first husband, Kogna

Holdbrook-Smith, both delivered amazing performances, even though it was eerie and disconcerting to witness someone who so accurately portrayed Ike's appearance and personality on screen.

Her concluding remarks to the crowd that first night, following a highly successful show in her honor, were as smart as they were revealing. They contained everything she had learned in her entire life, a life of terrifying terrible agony as well as wonderful blessings beyond her wildest expectations. She remembered an old Buddhist proverb: it is possible to turn poison into medicine.

Sometimes it seems like that single very spiritual sentence contains the entire story of her entire existence. What's next? Tina: The Musical will make its Broadway debut in New York in the fall of 2019. And, as another of her favorite Sinatra songs once suggested, if she can get there, she can get anyplace. And, once again, she delivered.

CHAPTER 9:
DRESS IN HEAVY WEATHER

Apart from my own personal interpretations and extensive listening to her entire musical arc, as well as speaking with so many fans, critics, journalists, and historians of both the soul and rock styles, it is abundantly clear that Tina Turner is exactly as Winston Churchill once described the inscrutable East: she is "a riddle, wrapped in a mystery, inside an enigma." Most importantly, and often overlooked, was his follow-up observation: perhaps there is a key. So many diverse sides to the same public persona: bashful but raucous, humble but pompous, meditative but manic.

Tina Turner had such a unique personality and character that she was practically a self-fulfilling prophecy—but in a good way. She was also that rare species of creature about whom all opinion and observation, even those that are completely diverse or diametrically opposed, are completely true. In other words, she was a figure whose creative shadow was so large that practically everything conflicting about her was equally true. Is there really a key?

Tina Turner was much more than a survivor; she was an alchemist who seemed to specialize in change. Turner's career, according to Victor Bockris, biographer of beat writer William Burroughs, is a series of metamorphosis. There is no such thing as a single Turner. And since there is plainly more than one of her, there must be more than one legacy. John Corcelli communicated to me his respect for her innate legacy in two ways: "her ability to embrace her own pain and to cultivate an ever expanding audience." Tina Turner should be recognized as a much-loved artist whose devoted fans were always rewarded with a fantastic performance."

True, we've already seen around four out of five Turners, and who knows how many more are on their way. That, too, is a significant part of her legacy: whatever she touched seemed to turn to gold. She made Ike Turner into gold and then went on to make her own solo songs into gold.

Legacy is such a heavy term. It can sound quite imperious at times. And yet, for someone as imperious as Tina Turner, it seems quite fitting. In a nutshell, what is her legacy? Tenacity—aside from the music and the presence of the person who gave it to us all as a collective gift: her refusal to be repressed, suppressed, or sad, and her refusal to ever give up. She didn't give up in her traumatic childhood, her horrible private relationship, the creative drought that followed her divorce, or even the life-threatening sickness that even someone as strong as she couldn't totally overcome. Throughout it all, she says, "I stayed on course."

Her perseverance will be remembered not only for how it affected her numerous admirers, but also for the impact it had on the whole music industry and her fellow musicians. Daphne Brooks studied the making of a rock-and-roll revolutionary in The Guardian in mid-2018 when she previewed a new live musical stage performance about the sixty-year career of a singer who bridged racial lines and braved violent tyranny to reinvent music. "Through singularity, Turner merged sound and movement at a watershed moment in rock history, navigating and reflecting back on the technological innovations of a new pop-music era in the late 1960s and early 1970s."

"She catapulted herself to the forefront of a musical revolution that had long marginalized and overlooked African-American women's pioneering contributions, then remade herself when most pop musicians were hitting the oldies circuit." Turner's persona has always been a powerful blend of mystery and light, melancholy coupled with a fiery vitality that frequently flirted with danger. Ideal for a big-budget musical."

Brooks also placed Turner's vast artistic shadow into context by naming people who probably wouldn't exist without her impact, reminding us that Turner's legacy extends far beyond Beyoncé and is rich and varied in the many worlds of music. From Meshell Ndegpcello's dark soul to white funk diva Nikka Costa and every time Rhianna enters the stage, to rapper Cardi B, they all owe Turner a massive debt of in-your-face female funk. Sisters are doing things for themselves, as the catchy feminist song implied.

When researching the "natural woman" that Tina Turner so vividly epitomizes, I've always enjoyed how Lucy O'Brien described it in her authoritative history of women in rock, pop, and soul, She Bop. "From Madonna's populist attack on Catholicism to Tina Turner strutting her survivalist ethic in stadiums around the world, a female assertion of identity within a male-dominated sphere is arguably an act of protest in and of itself."

That opinion is tempting because it implies that she is a protesting folksinger, even if she is unaware of it, simply by being herself. "People like me not just because I have big hair, lips, and legs," O'Brien pointed out, quoting Turner from her own feminist perspective. I have credibility!" She does, fighting for her own independence and freedom, refusing to back down. "It wasn't until British designer/pop producer Heaven 17 convinced her to record a cover version of 'Ball of Confusion' for their 1981 nostalgia compilation album that she realized she could make the transition from oldies soul (on her cabaret circuit) to a more commercial sound, wrapping her raunch and emotional vocal style around such anthems as 'What's Love Got to Do with It?' as well as 'We Don't Need Another Hero.'"

O'Brien refers to Tina Turner as a female pharaoh, a Hatshepsut (an Egyptian queen) taking her throne, in a brilliant section of her book about soul and funk queens. "Turner has various weapons at her disposal, including a horse's constitution, excellent legs, and a solid history in filthy r&b. This is accompanied by a preference for lion's mane and ridiculously crimson lipstick. Turner is well aware that she is a ham and that this is show business. It was the gospel-derived dynamics of deep southern soul, a gritty gutsy genre driven by Stax-label performers such as Carla Thomas and Mavis Staples, that went deeper than the girl-group sound. These musicians, together with blues singer Etta James, opened the way for full-throated stars like Tina Turner."

I've always thought Christian Wright's interpretation of her vocal chords in Trouble Girls captured her spirit. "She has that voice, completely unique, organic but unnamed, as if it had been left off the elements' table." She happened by chance. Her voice still sounds like freedom." Turner is aware that her voice isn't always "beautiful" or even "good." She can sound nice when she wants to, but she's long realized that's not what people want from her: they want her to sound as raspy as possible. She'd evidently found early on that she could be a gorgeous rock chick while also being a free and emancipated woman.

Ellen Willis, a great assessor of the politics of that social liberation wave that still sought the right to rock, presented another angle of approach to give her context in the women's movement that flourished during her middle years. Willis wryly commented astutely in response to Karen Durbin's question in Ms. magazine about whether a feminist can adore the world's best rock-and-roll band, "I try to explain that love didn't preclude tension and conflict." My own personal theme was the bleeding crossroads of rock and feminism: a sense of entitlement to grasp the world, free of the traditional feminine dictum, "thou shalt not offend."

That sensibility precisely coincides with what Turner may have been seeking for herself, again without being fully cognizant of the social aspect of her intrinsic and frequently disguised feminism. "Music that boldly and aggressively laid out what the singer wanted, loved, and hated—as good rock and roll did—challenged us to do the same, and encouraged my liberation struggle." Where women's liberation and musical liberty collide: rock and roll as a catalyst for utopian inspiration in a society that could be."

These insights (along with a few others) will assist us in locating Turner's legacy on the dramatically redrawn map of 1980s music in general, and women's roles in it in particular. They enable us to reimagine how powerfully she must have appeared to be coming into her own, just when the rest of society was finally ready to completely embrace her heavy-duty assertion of herself. It's also an angle that Christian Wright covered brilliantly in Trouble Girls, a book that was primarily a record of the distaff side in heavy rock and even punk circles.

"She definitely blazed a trail," Wright said, "but her voice echoes far beyond genre: Private Dancer, the 1984 hit-filled album that marked her renaissance, had flashes of rock and roll, but it's really a perfect pop record made with synthesizers and various producers." Songs, on the other hand, are practically secondary to Turner. 'What's Love Got to Do with It?' in the hands of anyone else.'would sound like the manufactured pop farce that it is, rather than the song of sexual emancipation that it has become."

However, I would reiterate that pop should be treated seriously, that it is a dark mirror, and that the best pop on earth (think of Brian Wilson's Pet Sounds or the Beatles' Revolver from 1966) is an excellent reflecting lens of the times as well as a magnificent piece of art.

"Never mind that she was forty-five years old when she made her comeback," Wright went on, "and that she competed in the pop marketplace with newcomers like Madonna and Sade, for whom she'd opened the door—she was already legendary." She'd become an icon for black people because she'd crossed over during segregation; for women because she'd achieved success in the mostly male field of music; and for herself because she'd survived it all."

Tina Turner's status as a feminist icon is now almost universally acknowledged. But this was not always the case. I recall Tina arriving on Ed Sullivan's Sunday-night variety program with her entire strutting Revue and the ominously swaying Ike, as do many of you who either witnessed it live or viewed later film. I also recollect thinking about what Gloria Steinem would have made of this spectacle: you've come a long way, baby—or not.

Tina was writhing around the stage in her small micro-mini skirt, occasionally performing her famous microphone massage act. She was unquestionably a paradox, one that Laurie Stras rightly identified as a "Bold Soul Trickster " in her She's So Fine research. Her Tina chapter title was, of course, a play on the title of one of her 1969 hits, "Bold Soul Sister," from the album The Hunter. I also remember thinking how amazing it must have been for primarily white middle-class audiences to be exposed to so much black woman-ness at once. In fact, I'm still surprised.

Her "Bold Soul Sister" wasn't one of their better efforts, mostly a channeling of the basic James Brown ethos pumped up with enough estrogen to suit her special vibe, but Stras's name change in her study of rock femininity is a telling indicator of two things for me: Tina's ironic status as a combination of conflicting images, both a hot rock chick turning on crowds and a towering feminist metaphor for surviving oppression. I've always believed she was a trickster because, as I've said, I believe she was mostly a female impersonator (not in a bad manner) who was posing as a character much at odds with her own shy and retiring nature, as difficult as that may be to swallow.

She would truly become a feminist icon only after her private life became well known and she ultimately left Ike. But, in my opinion, she truly took the mantle of female icon only when she had also shed the title of rhythm-and-blues singer (she was never really a soul singer anyway) and after she had also shed the label of rock singer. I believe she ascended to the throne of feminist icon by accident, owing to her status as a certified pop star who crossed all ethnic and gender lines—a planetary-style citizen.

After all, in her last spectacular performance, at England's Wembley Stadium in 2000, she was still flanked by a new batch of her song and dance girls, all around a third her age and still slithering while step dancing across the stage. But something had changed in her, something that had irreversibly transformed her soul since she originally performed that exact same act (more or less) in her early show business days forty years ago. Then it was at the request and direction of her boss, but now she was and still is (as Aretha and Annie's feminist anthemic pop song goes) a sister doing it for herself. Laurie Stras opined sharply on femininity in pop and rock music, examining how the male maestro needs to make even more behind-the-scenes claims of credit and control in order to co opt or reduce the function of embodied voices on stage or in the recording studio. "This was evidenced by the Revue's increasingly acclaimed innovative sounds and performances, which were frequently downplayed as a result of his supposed creative brilliance rather than Tina's obvious significance." Thus, Ike's power over Tina and the Ikettes was always a familiar scenario of women's agency being diluted."

As Jacqueline Warwick points out in Girl Groups, Girl Culture, the majority of female musicians must cope with the implicit assumption that the men in their lives are the true builders of their success. Warwick has approached the problem from a perspective that allows her to place the bodies making the music in the center rather than on the periphery of this dynamic equation. That insight is critical to understanding the age-old Svengali scenario, the notion that he created her look and movements (aside from the obvious ability he had in recognizing her innate skills as a young woman), but, as that author so ably pointed out, "it is Tina who materialized these extraordinary elements of her performances."

She also stated that Tina's "embodied voice, her physical presence on stage, her costumed moving body are what draw the eye, heart, and soul." Perhaps that's why, despite his desire to control the show, Ike was so profoundly frustrated with her," she concluded. Warwick has clearly identified Tina as a signifier, a symbol that conveys meaning through her actions, stating that "this gives her tremendous agency and control over her career (real or imagined)," because "no matter what material she is given to sing, no matter what musicians she works with, it is the very materiality of her voice that defines her."

Tina's voice has always had an inherent hard but aching quality to it that has always identified her with the mostly male-modeled rock and roll she has always represented: a bigness, a rawness, and a hard-edged assertiveness that is aggressive and demanding but also feminine, if slightly strained and choked. Her power is hidden in that duality.

So much so, in my opinion, that it was in her later post-Ike rock and pop material that she gradually and ironically donned that feminist crown, albeit still wearing her exploding red wigs and miniskirts teetering perilously on dangerously gorgeous stilettos. True, she is still what she was back then: an embodied meaning.

The other term that comes to mind when I think about Tina Turner is "serendipity," which is the operation of meaningful coincidence in our lives that psychologist Carl Jung referred to as synchronicity. Of course, someone with Buddhist Tina's intellectual or spiritual bent would call it by its more colloquial name: karma. But let's keep with serendipity because it sounds less frightening and possibly a little more cheerful.

It was coincidence that her broken-up family moved to St. Louis, and serendipity that she followed shortly after and happened to walk into a certain nightclub with a hot rhythm-and-blues band performing. It was serendipity for her to get up and sing along without any formal training, and it was also serendipity for her to be forced by violence into an independent career she may not have had if her musical partner had simply been a nicer guy. It was also a serendipitous meeting with someone who taught her the Buddhist spiritual practice that she credits with saving her life at the time. That strikes me as supersized serendipity.

The mystery quarrel with Elton John that derailed a planned joint concert tour together was even an exotic sort of serendipity that she ended up making her final solo album and going on a smash final tour. Initially, she planned to tour with Elton, and a joint project was in the works, but their fateful meeting at the Divas Live event changed everything. Tina stopped the music during a band rehearsal and went over to tell Elton how she believed a certain piece should be played. Boom.

It didn't take long for her to realize she'd made a mistake by thinking she needed to show him how to play "Proud Mary." The error was that you didn't show Elton John how to play his piano. He just flew into a frenzy and declared that it was wrong. It was. The combined tour plans were scrapped, and Turner went straight into the studio to make her final album, which might not have been made had it not been for the transgression that triggered their argument. Ironically, the alleged problems she was in at the time was caused by what? By wishing for the piano music to be appropriate for the song she was singing?

Perhaps a little of sour serendipity, but it resulted in an entire unexpected album and a massive unscheduled final tour that would not have happened otherwise. Meanwhile, on her way into the studio to record her final Twenty Four Seven album, she stopped by the Super Bowl pregame show to perform "Proud Mary" live. Just to warm up. Lots of guts.

She had an awareness that had been with her since the beginning about what performing meant to her in general and what she anticipated her final gigs would feel like personally. She realizes it's all a performance. She's performing in a short movie for that brief instant in time. That's why, as watchers, everything of the activity and interplay between her and her girls seemed so natural. For those two hours, it's like being onstage in real life. Even though she had been playing that part for nearly half a century—and perhaps even herself suspecting that she should hang up her dancing shoes—she was thrilled to do it all again because she recognizes she is at heart a living incarnation of rock and roll. She desired that others see her at her best.

But, given we're dealing with Tina Turner, she naturally has a different definition of the word "retirement" than most other individuals. She didn't so much disobey the rules as she refused to acknowledge the existence of any rules to break. Her eventual exit from public life would be as gradual and steady as her entrance. When asked by Vanity Fair magazine what her life mantra was and how she kept going, she replied, "I put my right foot forward."

In some ways, as she approached her swan song, she must have been looking forward to simply being Anna Mae Bullock again and not having to imitate Tina any longer—or, as she put it, to play that role in a short movie onstage virtually every night. But another part of her had already become Tina forever, and that's the part that would always naturally prevail, as we'd all see soon enough—until it was all gone for real, until the encores stopped.

Being Anna Mae Bullock again did not mean returning to Nutbush in the literal sense, though as I've mentioned, because Nutbush had no city lines, she never truly left it at all; rather, she brought it with her wherever she went. Meanwhile, Tennessee State Route 19, the little escape route highway between Brownsville and Nutbush, was formally dubbed "Tina Turner Highway" in 2002, maybe to inspire any other citizen with similarly lofty ambitions to take the road.

Other legacy distinctions would quickly follow, including the aforementioned Kennedy Center Honor, at which her close friend Oprah Winfrey complimented her with this heartfelt introduction: "We don't need another hero, but we do need more heroines like you, Tina." You make me happy to spell my name with the letters w-o-m-a-n!"

In 2007, she became affiliated with the Beyond Foundation, a Swiss-based nonprofit interfaith spiritual organization formed to assist projects that unite cultures throughout the world via music in order to foster mutual religious respect and spiritual understanding. Their mission was to sow seeds for a more compassionate world through projects, proposals, events, concerts, mentorship, and personal growth tools. She is still devoting her time and energy to this social and cultural cause that is dear to her heart.

River: The Joni Letters, a Herbie Hancock album released in 2007, included Turner as well as Leonard Cohen, Norah Jones, Corinne Bailey Rae, Lucian Souza, and Joni Mitchell. "Edith and the Kingpin," a song by Joni Mitchell from her experimental album The Hissing of Summer Lawns (1975), was her vocal contribution.

River: The Joni Letters received a Grammy Award for album of the year in 2008, with Tina gladly sharing honors as a featured artist. And, perhaps unsurprisingly given all of my comments about the déjà vu nature of her retirement, 2008 witnessed the incredible appearance of a special series of concerts: Tina! Tina!, the 50th Anniversary Tour, was a suitably spectacular and super-successful celebration that, predictably, was complemented by an equally festive record., a collection of previous hits. This would descend on the world in October of that year, cementing the superstar's legacy after fifty great years in the show industry.

Its genesis was also heavily influenced by chance. This was eight years after Twenty Four Seven, her ostensibly final album and tour, and she was blissfully "retired" from both music and traveling at the time. She was even missing from much of a public life by that point, at least by her old spotlight standards. Friends and peers alike began to murmur about the fact that she'd been an entertainer for half a century, literally, since first joining Ike in St. Louis and then finally putting away her dancing shoes for a well-deserved period of reflection.

But, of course, that break didn't last long, and she quickly announced yet another landmark tour, claiming that the inspiration came during a fashion show in Milan where she was seated next to Sophia Loren, another long-term queen like herself. Loren apparently objected when Tina informed her that she was taking a break, insisting that the break was over because people wanted to see her—needed to see her. So it was time to return to her one and only true job: making people happy. She immediately called her agency and proclaimed that it was time to get back to work.

After the enormous response to her Grammy appearance, Tina promptly decided to use the event to honor the formal history of her career, dating back to her first official engagement at the Club Imperial with the Kings of Rhythm in 1958. She also stated that she wanted the tour, which was announced in May 2008, to begin in Missouri because that is where it all began for her. The show itself would be videotaped for a DVD movie called Tina Live, and tickets sold out in minutes.

Tina Live's stage production was incredibly elaborate, incorporating dramatic design aspects from many of her previous famous events. It began with "Steamy Windows" and ended with an encore finale of "Nutbush City Limits" (after "Proud Mary" had inevitably completed the set list). Both critics and fans praised the film. The Washington Post labeled her a force to be reckoned with, while Rolling Stone described her as polished and soulful but in the old-fashioned way: lovely and rugged.

According to Tom Horan of the Sunday Telegraph, "Turner demonstrated why she is still regarded as a Goddess in Europe." If you have to say what the feeling is you're left with with Turner, it's a feeling of triumph: I've come this far, I've done it, I'm still standing." Perhaps most importantly, Ian Gittins of The Guardian noted that "crucially, her voice has not been in the least bit damaged by her long layoff," while The Observer's Euan Ferguson exclaimed, "It was a moment of perfect triumph: for the grit and feathers of"To which he added a unique caveat: "What does age have to do with it?" "There is nothing."

But perhaps Billboard's Jonathan Cohen articulated what we were all thinking. "The point is, this woman defies so much conventional wisdom that being in her presence for two and a half hours is a bit of a mental trip!'"

While she was "resting up" after her tour and album release in 2009, the Beyond Foundation she had formed with like-minded spiritual friends released the first of several CDs, albums of interfaith music, chants, and songs featuring Turner, Tibetan Buddhist Dechen Shak-Dagsay, and Christian singer Regula Curti. Thus began Tina Turner's unexpected post-pop era.

BEYOND: BUDDHIST AND CHRISTIAN PRAYERS 2010

Tina Turner, Regula Curti, and Dechen Shak-Dagsay star in this Beyond Foundation production. The video lasts 90:00 minutes. It included Tibetan Tara chants and lyrics from the medieval abbess Hildegard of Bingen, as well as interfaith meditative and prayer techniques and the mystical poetry of the Persian poet Rumi. Attending a ceremony on interreligious dialogue hosted in 2005 by the Dalai Lama and Martin Werlen, head of the Benedictine abbey Einsiedeln Abbey in Einsiedeln, Switzerland, inspired all of the Beyond Foundation's founding members.

BEYOND: CHILDREN/CHORAL MEDITATIVE WORKS, 2011

The Beyond Foundation's second music album features the founders with over thirty children from various cultures throughout the world. The video lasts 60:00 minutes.

BEYOND: LOVE WITHIN/BUDDHIST, CHRISTIAN, AND HINDU PRAYERS FOR 2014

Sawani Shende-Sathaye, an additional singer, was added to the Beyond Foundation's third release, and their common repertoire was broadened to include Hindu chants and songs. "Singing takes you beyond hatred, fear, and revenge," they say of their music. ..Underneath the unpleasant emotions, you find yourself in a field where love and serenity reign."

BEYOND: AWAKENING IN 2017

Kareem Roustom (iGroove) produced and created the track. Tina's Beyond Foundation's fourth CD has six different singers from six distinct nations. Rugula Curti (Switzerland), Ani Choying (Nepal), Dimi Orsho (Syria, United States), Sawani Shende Sathaye (India), and More Karbasi (Israel) perform lyrics, prayers, and lullabies. Turner delivers a spiritual message of unity. The London Philharmonic Orchestra performed on the soundtrack, which was recorded at the renowned Abbey Road Studios. The time is 140:00.
Is this your typical pop rock superstar's retirement life?

Dealing with someone as unique as Tina Turner can feel like "loading mercury with a pitchfork," as poet Richard Brautigan once cryptically described it. Madame Mercury has said, "She's not only different from so many other artists of her era(s), she's also different from herself at various stages of her own career, and is constantly morphing into her next slippery incarnation."

Readers occasionally ask how I've worked with so many completely different and diverse female singers and songwriters, artists who don't appear to have anything in common on the surface. A good question, and one I frequently ask myself. After writing books about Amy Winehouse, Sharon Jones, and Tina Turner, as well as chapters in other books about Marianne Faithfull, Stevie Nicks, and Joni Mitchell, it occurred to me that they all have something in common. However, it might be something subterranean that is shared by all of their personas and work. For one thing, they all strike me as powerful empaths: creatures capable of profound emotional perception: of receiving and transmitting sentiments through their own personas and projecting them back outward to the world at large. In a very real way, because of this shared quality, they appear to be able to channel deeply universal feelings, so deep that we frequently believe they are speaking directly to or about us, almost as if they were mediums— which they are.

Despite their outward look of invincibility, such a power makes the empath exceedingly delicate and susceptible. And, sure, Tina Turner, despite her obvious tenacity as a survivor, is just as frail and susceptible as most other empaths on a personal level. She simply manages to navigate or compensate for her fragility, to rise above it time and again, to give voice to all of us who feel delicate or even injured. As a result, her music became a kind of curative elixir, both for her and for the rest of us.

Tina Turner's professional and personal life were, as usual, an embarrassment of triumphant riches and a painful cauldron of mixed blessings: in January 2018, it was announced that Turner would receive a Grammy Lifetime Achievement Award, and in October of the same year, the musical Tina premiered to positive reviews in England, followed the following year by the bright lights of Broadway, where the lamb lies down. Yet, whether blessings or trials, nothing ever seemed to come easy for her: in July 2018, her first son, Craig (fathered by her partner Raymond Hill but later adopted by Ike Turner), was discovered dead by suicide from a self-inflicted gunshot wound.

But, just as she had handled her own painful illness with grace and dignity, she handled the sadness of losing her son with the same. Turner faced Craig's death in a very philosophical manner, much as she had refused to feel depressed after rising from her hospital bed and falling flat on her face to the floor, instead deciding she would somehow remedy her position. In the midst of a lifetime of chronic violence and upheaval, which she had long accepted as her karma in this life but not necessarily her life story, she made it an act of sheer willpower to conclude her story on her own terms. This included wondering if something in her son's life, that chaotic existence they both experienced with her first husband, had followed him like a shadow, weighing on him until he couldn't take it any longer.

She even bravely determined that her son was most likely now in a better place, a good place, a place where he was supposed to be. Tina Turner was in keeping with the dynamic energy and spirit that had led her to where she was, and even then, despite all her recent health and wellness issues. Despite everything she's been through in a life full of ups and downs and ups, she still believes she's exactly where she's supposed to be.

Sounds like a rare form of contentment and tranquility. But consider the paradox. She has accepted both her enormous accomplishments and her own death, even accepting her own son's premature departure and the knowledge that she herself has fewer days ahead of her than behind her. And yet, fifty-three years after famously singing Phil Spector's rather odd song about a little rag doll while sitting by her placid Lake Zurich, she heard it sung again on the radio in February 2018 in a new single release by Adrienne Warren from the cast album of the musical extravaganza based on her extraordinary life.

And then it all came rushing back into the present, like though caught in a time warp. Even though all or many of her wishes have already come true, even if it has been a long, laborious process, she still had to relive many of the more difficult portions of her story when it was presented on Broadway in late 2019, and so, yes, it's déjà vu all over again. But it must have felt more like jamais vu ("never seen"). The two main goals she set for herself were to be acknowledged as the genuine talent behind the Ike and Tina Turner Revue, which debuted so boisterously in 1960, and to find her true love with a loving and generous partner in Erwin Bach.

The strange thing about dreamers is that they never stop dreaming; it's as natural to them as breathing. And I'm reminded of a phrase used as one of the titles by the famous American poet Delmore Schwartz: in dreams begin responsibilities. Tina Turner's contributions to our collective dream have reminded us all of what we can dream and that we also have a responsibility to make happen—that to gamble with life is to give it value, and that even if the true meaning of life is that it ends and is found in its impermanence, the true purpose of life is to somehow make that impermanence itself meaningful.

So, like the rest of her narrative, Turner seemed to embrace the need for her society to celebrate her once more in a live musical biography with the same calm and contentment. Okay, good with me, because we're all now admiring her narrative together and sharing our collective affection for an amazing woman. By slightly modifying those Spector lyrics, we can say, "Our love has grown, and it gets stronger in every way, and it gets deeper, and it gets higher, day by day."

Still, hearing "River Deep, Mountain High" resounding from the rafters of a Broadway theater must be unusual for her, with another young singer, Adrienne Warren, striving to channel her own inner Tina in order to do that grand song proper honor. According to the editors of Qweerist, Turner was satisfied with the theatrical results: "Tali Pelman, Producer of Tina: The Musical commented that 'River Deep, Mountain High' is a pivotal moment in our show." It needs not only exceptional talent, but also enormous enthusiasm and bravery."

Tina Turner told them about that pivotal 1966 song, saying, "At that very difficult time in my life, recording this song opened my eyes to many possibilities." I felt emancipated, enthusiastic, and ready to confront myself verbally. It showed me how I wanted to sing in the future. I am overjoyed that Adrienne has taken up the mantle and not only met the challenge, but has also made this scene one of my favorites in the musical. It's only fitting that this is the first song from our upcoming cast album."
Turner was being overly nice and generous as usual, because the Warren version, as serious and really evocative as it is, doesn't even come close to matching the impact of the original—for one hilarious reason: Warren has a polished and normal-sounding voice. As usual,

it's difficult to find the perfect words to describe Tina's quivering mouth's dry, gritty howl fifty-three years ago. Nonetheless, the musical was unquestionably a final and lasting tribute to a natural force, a legacy of pure love.

It was directed by Phyllida Lloyd and choreographed by Anthony van Laast, with set and costume design by Mark Thompson and musical supervision by Nicholas Skilbeck, lighting by Bruno Poet, sound by Nevin Steinberg, projection by Jeff Sugg, and orchestrations by Ethan Popp. Ghostlight Records published the show's cast album in October 2019.

"Working on this show has been a life-changing experience for me," Tony-nominated (for Shuffle Along and Bring It On) main actress Adrienne Warren told Greg Evans of Deadline. Tina's unwavering courage, grace, and tenacity have been a constant source of inspiration, and I am grateful for the opportunity to be a part of relaying her story. This show is a dream come true." So we have another youthful dreamer that matches the overall tone of our Tina story nicely. P.S. She also has the right legs for the job!

Michael Billington's April 2018 Guardian essay also catches some of Tina's turmoil, describing it as a "whirlwind Turner tribute that leaves you breathless in a heady celebration of triumph over adversity with an astonishing turn by the young singer." The fact that the show is totally dependent on Warren, who is rarely offstage and is simply amazing, is especially noteworthy. "Above all, she captures the fact that there are multiple Tina Turners, how she grows and changes, and how, as she transitions to rock stardom, she retains her ferocious energy while introducing occasional notes of pungent melancholy." Warren portrays Tina's transformation from a stoic victim to a woman of fierce confidence. As far as bio-musicals go, this is the best."

Tina Turner's unique brand of optimistic hopefulness is, indeed, as wonderful as it gets. Her trademark optimism, however, had a fragile side, as she admitted with candor in My Love Story, revealing that she occasionally thought death was tapping her on the shoulder and heralding its approach. The ability to look at everything through the prism of mortality, which may have been learned during the course of a rich and fruitful life, is the opposite side of that spooky sense. She has the ability to skillfully reflect on the past, gratefully consider what it means to live in the present, and optimistically consider the future.

Despite her acute awareness that life is not only transient and impermanent, but also startlingly fleeting, whenever she is asked (as she frequently is) whether there is anything else she still wants in life, she unfailingly confirms what we have always suspected: she has everything. She sits by Lake Zurich in her dream home with her dream spouse, unable to help but feel at peace. Yes, she's had a difficult life, but she never blamed anything or anyone during her long and prosperous life. She appears to have enough compassion, and perhaps this is due to the Buddhist foundation she upholds, to live her life on her own terms. She made it through it all. And she appears to be a very happy person.

She has earned the right to want to do nothing after accomplishing everything she set out to do in her life, which makes her autumn encounter with New York Times reporter Amanda Hess all the more endearing. Hess described Turner's current situation as "Tina Turner is Having the Time of Her Life: a Swiss chateau, a Broadway musical all about her, and absolutely nothing she has to do." A big part of the charming part was the metal plaque on the gate to Turner's estate that says, "Vor 12.00 Uhr nicht lauten, keine Lieferungen," which Hess interpreted as "Do not even think about bothering Tina Turner before noon."

Hess perfectly captured the occasion. "For 50 years, she was a symbol of rock and roll endurance." She became a star with Ike Turner in her twenties, escaped his brutality in her thirties, clawed her way up the pop charts in her forties, toured the world until her sixties, and now she wants to sleep in late." She has been retired for ten years and, as Hess described it, is "basking in all of the nothing she has to do."

Yes, Turner is enjoying her well-deserved retirement, claiming that she was simply weary of singing and making other people happy, which she has done her entire life. Even if she isn't singing much these days, Tina has a slew of Tinas performing on her behalf all over the world. Tina Turner: The Musical introduced Tina to London, Hamburg, and Broadway. When asked if it was uncomfortable to watch all these other women try to be her, she replied that she had spent her entire career watching other women pretend to be her. In fact, when she was auditioning girls to be Ikettes in the Revue a lifetime ago, she would frequently observe this or that worried expectant that she'd make a fine Tina.

In fact, Hess commented that when Turner became tired of talking about herself, something she's also spent a career doing, the journalist left her for a bit, and when she returned the next afternoon, the actress had been transformed: wig groomed, lips painted red, eyes gleaming. "That was Anna Mae yesterday," she explained to Hess. "Here's Tina today." She also startled Hess by saying that after being a symbol of so many things—sex appeal, resilience, and empowerment—the thought of tying her life to the feminist movement or recasting it via the current MeToo campaign is something alien to her. She only identified with her own life because, while everyone else was busy turning her into a symbol, she was just living it. But she has a legacy written all over her.

Somewhere along the way, Anna Mae Bullock seems to have discovered something that dramatist G. B. Shaw once said, "Life is not about finding yourself, it's not about finding anything at all, it's only about creating yourself." She'd been doing that since the beginning, and she's succeeded in her chosen life by continuing to create and re-create Tina Turner. Even after all of her ups and downs, she eventually built a truly happy Anna Mae Bullock.

Printed in Great Britain
by Amazon

32548324R00109